AF413141

SITUATIONAL LEADERSHIP®

THE MODEL *for* LEADING OTHERS, NAVIGATING CHANGE, *and* UNLOCKING PERFORMANCE

SAM SHRIVER | SUZIE BISHOP

FOREWORD BY CHRIS McLEAN

www.amplifypublishinggroup.com

Situational Leadership®: The Model for Leading Others, Navigating Change, and Unlocking Performance

For more information, please contact:
Amplify Publishing, an imprint of Amplify Publishing Group
620 Herndon Parkway, Suite 100
Herndon, VA 20170
info@amplifypublishing.com

Library of Congress Control Number: 2026907837

CPSIA Code: PRFRE0426A

ISBN-13: 979-8-89138-838-3

Printed in Canada

To the more than fifteen million learners, practitioners, and trainers of the Situational Leadership® Model—you've carried this approach into training rooms, one-on-one meetings, boardrooms, and communities across the globe, proving every day that leadership is something you do with others. Your commitment has turned a framework into a legacy that continues to shape how the world leads.

Contents

Foreword

It's a privilege to introduce *Situational Leadership®: The Model for Leading Others, Navigating Change, and Unlocking Performance*, a book that brings to life the timeless principles of the Situational Leadership® Model in a practical, relevant, and deeply impactful way.

For more than half a century, the Situational Leadership® Model has served as one of the most enduring and adaptable frameworks in the field of leadership development. Built on the belief that leadership is not defined by a single style but by a person's ability to respond to the needs of others, it's guided millions of leaders through the complexities of growth, change, and human motivation. The genius of the model lies in its simplicity. Because it's a model and not a theory, it's clear, actionable, and pragmatic in every type of organization and culture.

I've had the pleasure of knowing Dr. Sam Shriver for many years. From his early years learning directly from Dr. Paul Hersey to his decades shaping the work of The Center for Leadership Studies, Sam has become one of the model's most trusted voices. His gift lies in taking rich, complicated theory and distilling it into something clear, practical, and accessible for leaders at every level. Sam's insight, humility, and steady wisdom have influenced the evolution of the Situational Leadership® framework in profound ways. And his commitment to helping leaders understand and apply these concepts continues to strengthen everything we do.

Suzie Bishop's journey is equally inspiring. From her early days at The Center for Leadership Studies to her role shaping its future, she's become a visionary force behind the modern evolution of Situational Leadership®—related products. Suzie's gift lies in making complex ideas practical and relevant for today's leaders. Her creativity, insight, and genuine care infuse this work with wisdom that feels both timeless and immediately useful.

Hersey often said that effective leadership is a function of many variables. He had the rare ability to simplify that complexity without losing its essence. Sam and Suzie carry that same spirit forward in these pages. They present the principal elements of the leadership equation with remarkable clarity so that any leader, from individual contributor to CEO, can apply the content immediately.

My own introduction to this model was transformational. I was raised in a results-oriented operational environment, "old school," where performance ruled and direction with a heavy hand was the standard. Early in my career, I had one leadership style in my tool kit: push hard, drive results, and stay relentlessly focused on outcomes. It worked for a while, but it wasn't sustainable. Four years into my leadership journey, I was introduced to the Situational Leadership® Model, and it completely reframed how I viewed leadership.

I came to understand that while I was achieving results, I wasn't creating engagement. I was driving performance but not developing people. This model taught me to flex my leadership style to meet people where they are rather than expecting them to adapt to my style. It showed me that effective leadership isn't about treating everyone the same; it's about providing the right balance of direction and support based on their readiness to perform a certain activity.

Decades later, as I continue to lead and coach leaders, I still rely on this framework to guide my conversations and decision-making. It's become more than a model—it's a mindset. Over the past thirty-seven years, I've had the privilege of sharing this approach with leaders across the world, helping them translate its principles into real, lasting impact. Since becoming certified in 2003—and later Master Certified by our founder, Dr. Hersey—I've witnessed its power in every context imaginable. To date I've trained tens of thousands of leaders and personally certified hundreds more, and I remain convinced:

The Situational Leadership® Model is as relevant today as the day it was created.

Leaders who embrace this modeldrive performance, build engagement, and navigate change with confidence. Even more, they become better coaches, mentors, and parents, as the skills learned naturally extend to every relationship in life.

In *Situational Leadership®: The Model for Leading Others, Navigating Change, and Unlocking Performance*, Sam and Suzie have created something truly special: a guide that is both instructive and inspiring. As you go through this book, I encourage you to do more than read—pause, reflect, and apply what you're learning to your own sphere of influence. You'll discover that this model—both classic and modern—has the power to transform not only how you lead but how you live.

Chris McLean

Vice President of Training and Global Master Trainer
The Center for Leadership Studies

Introduction

Margot was recently promoted to sales manager for a small software company. She had a long track record of personal results, exceptional experience in mentoring new salespeople, and a strong recommendation from her previous manager. In her first week, the executive team was impressed. She seemed poised to lead the team to a great year of sales.

But as time went on, Margot began to struggle. By nature she was comfortable providing structure, background, and direction and then getting out of the way. She'd gather the team, unload a slew of details, and immediately ask if anybody had any questions as they stared back, stunned and wide-eyed. They were drowning, but Margot assumed their silence meant they had what they needed.

So she didn't check in. She didn't encourage or initiate discussion. She didn't follow up. Most of the team had been in their roles for a while, so she assumed they could manage. In her mind she had equipped them, and it was time for them to take action. When someone finally mustered up the courage to ask for clarity, Margot responded with visible frustration and irritation, as if she couldn't believe they didn't already get it.

Within a few weeks, it was clear no one felt safe going to her for help, and performance was slipping. For a variety of reasons, no one wanted to admit they felt abandoned—so they pressed on. The most experienced salesperson set his own pace and encouraged the rest of the team to make their calls. But the newer team members, who were still learning the ropes, struggled to hit even the minimum goals. Performance declined enough that Margot was called into the executive offices twice.

Surprisingly, the two newest hires would tell you Margot was the best leader they'd ever had. She stayed close to them and monitored their progress, and when they struggled, she'd jump on their calls, take over, and close the deals for them. It helped in the moment but also created different problems—insecurity and dependency.

No one else on the team received that kind of hands-on attention and coaching, even though every person on the team was committed and willing to learn. They made adjustments whenever Margot asked, especially after her meetings with the executives. But they continued to struggle with the excessive number of details Margot provided and languished without the support they didn't know how to ask for.

One Style Doesn't Fit All

Books, classes, and many leadership advisers seem to think that good leadership means consistently executing a certain set of behaviors over time. Of course, they all seem to fight over which behaviors are the right ones. But they all tend to think a single style is best.

Margot is a great example of where this assumption goes wrong.

Her approach was highly consistent. It worked well with the newest salespeople for a while, who needed step-by-step instruction. And her "empowerment" approach was perfectly fine for the most senior salesperson, who had thirty years of experience and was dedicated to his craft.

But the same behaviors didn't work for Margot with the rest of the team—not at all. The majority of the department felt alone and unsupported after she left them to handle situations on their own. Eventually, several of them resigned and accepted other opportunities. And when the newest salespeople had integrated and were no longer being officially onboarded, they, too, began to feel abandoned and miserable. Their performance, which had initially been moving in a positive direction, began to stall out too.

Margot's struggles aren't uncommon. In fact, you have probably worked with a Margot or maybe even been a Margot yourself. The problem isn't even with (most of) the behaviors Margot was displaying in this example; her style worked beautifully for the newest and the most skilled employees. The problem was how inflexible that style became.

That's because, as you'll learn in the pages to come, no single leadership style works for every situation. Like Margot, most leaders rely on an approach that feels natural to them, but it doesn't always match what the specific moment requires. The key is learning to recognize what each situation calls for and adapt your approach accordingly. Without that ability, it's easy to fall into the same trap.

Now, for a moment, put yourself into the shoes of a follower. As an employee, you'd probably say you want a boss who recognizes and adjusts to your level of skill and confidence.

Imagine you're brand new at a job. You don't know what you're doing, and you feel intimidated. But your manager confidently takes charge of your onboarding and tells you what to do and how to do it, every step of the way. All you have to do is follow her lead. How would that feel?

Now imagine you're at the other end of the spectrum, working in a profession you've excelled at for years. You love doing your job. You take pride in knowing every detail of what to do and in doing it well. Your manager deeply respects your mastery, is there whenever you need him, and makes it clear he trusts you. Day by day you come into work, and he largely leaves you alone to work autonomously.

Now imagine you're somewhere in between. You're good at the basics of your job, but you struggle when something changes unexpectedly (which happens often, by the way). When you reach out to your manager, she's always there to help. Her advice makes the solution clear to you, and her encouragement helps you relax and feel confident that you can work your way through the approach she suggests. As you get better at your job over time, she begins to give you more leeway to figure things out on your own, but she's always just a message away.

On the other hand, how would you feel if your manager tried to tell you every detail of a job you'd been doing for years? Or if he left you alone instead of onboarding you and assumed you'd figure out a brand-new job without help? That likely would feel as troubling as the right match of behaviors felt helpful. Hopefully you're starting to see the point here—the impact you have as a leader directly depends on your ability to match the follower's needs in that particular moment.

Simplifying the Leadership Equation

Leadership is complex. When someone takes on a management role for the first time, they may be confident in their technical abilities but quickly realize that leading is about much more than doing the work themselves. It requires influencing others to deliver results, and that shift introduces layers of complexity that can feel absolutely overwhelming.

Our founder, Dr. Paul Hersey, understood that challenge well. He knew leadership effectiveness is never shaped by just one factor but by a constellation of influences. He captured the big picture in the following simple expression:

Le = f(S); (F); (B); (A); (P); (C) . . .

In this equation, effective leadership (Le) is a function of (f) many variables.

- **S: The Situation**—The task at hand and its context
- **F: The Follower**—Their ability and willingness for this task
- **B: Your Boss**—The guidance or pressure you receive from above
- **A: Other Associates**—Peers who influence you, your team, and the work
- **P: Organizational Performance**—Success, stress, and urgency all play a part
- **C: Company Culture**—Expectations, norms, and what "good" looks like

You could add so many more—market forces, technology, resource constraints, life circumstances, you name it. The point is, leadership doesn't happen in a vacuum; everything around us has the potential to shape how we show up and what we're able to achieve.

The goal is not to master every variable. You couldn't, even if you tried. Instead, Hersey used this equation to illustrate both the complexity of leadership and our natural desire to make sense of it. When we attempt to account for every factor, it's easy to become overwhelmed and lose focus on what we can actually influence.

This is why the simplicity of the Situational Leadership® Model is so powerful. While acknowledging that effective leadership involves many forces, Hersey emphasized an essential truth: If the follower decides not to follow, the other variables become inconsequential. You may have an ideal strategy, a supportive boss, and a healthy culture, but if the person responsible for carrying out that particular task isn't able or willing to do it, you're not going to get very far.

Because of that, the model concentrates on the two areas where leaders have the greatest opportunity to make an impact: the situation and the follower. Everything else still plays a role, and those factors will always contribute to how a leader thinks and behaves. But at the core, leadership rests on understanding what needs to be done, who's doing it, and how to align those two pieces in a way that creates momentum.

The model doesn't claim to solve every leadership challenge or address every variable in the broader equation. Instead, it offers a practical starting point. When leaders learn to assess the task at hand and the readiness of the person performing it, they gain a foundation that can flex and grow as new complexities arise. From there, they can begin to layer in additional factors—organizational dynamics, relationships with peers, cultural norms, and their own personal approach—to deepen their influence.

A Simple, Practical Framework

The developers of Situational Leadership® took hundreds of studies in leadership and organizational behavior and integrated them into a commonsense framework that helps leaders drive performance. They identified the key factors that determine effective leadership, based on decades of that pioneering research, and then put them into a model that's straightforward enough and practical enough to use every single day, in every single situation.

Here's what you need to be a Situational Leader:

- Clarity (with your follower) on the task
- Alignment (with your follower) on their ability and willingness to perform the task
- Flexibility (with your style) to adapt your approach and meet the needs of others
- Understanding (of the environment) that no situation ever stays the same

Sometimes people object to the simplicity of this model, arguing that leadership is more than a set of simple steps. For the record we *emphatically* agree! There will always be nuance and exceptions. People and workplaces are complex, and as a result, adapting to those complexities takes intentional effort and practice.

But regardless of all those complexities, starting with the right foundation makes all the difference. The Situational Leadership® Model allows you to take all the information around you and boil it down into actionable steps. You can identify the kind of response that makes success most likely in the situation you're facing. From there you can customize your approach to the personal and external circumstances as appropriate.

For more than five decades, the Situational Leadership® Model has stood the test of time, helping leaders across industries and cultures build trust, navigate change, and drive performance in every facet of their jobs and lives. Today's leaders face new challenges: hybrid teams, rapid change, and a constant demand for agility. This book brings the enduring power of the model into modern terms, showing how its principles apply just as strongly in today's complex, fast-moving world as they did when it was first introduced.

We'll begin by grounding leadership in influence. We'll explore how that influence shows up in everyday life and why understanding human behavior is key to leading well. From there, the Situational

Leadership® Model comes into view. You'll learn how readiness works, how leadership styles take shape, and how decades of research formed the backbone of this approach. These early chapters build the foundation every leader needs to apply the model with clarity and confidence.

> **❝** *There will always be a task to accomplish, a person (even if assisted) responsible for it, and a leader guiding the process.*

Then we'll turn to practice. We'll walk step-by-step through the Situational Leadership® process—how to identify a task, assess Performance Readiness®, and respond with the right leadership approach for the situation. You'll learn how to communicate with intention, manage movement, drive performance, and navigate change in a way that keeps people informed, engaged, and growing. By the end you'll see how flexible, responsive leadership empowers people to succeed—and how Situational Leadership® equips you to lead anyone, anywhere, through anything.

You'll finish this book with a clear understanding you can immediately turn into action. From that foundation, you'll make more intentional decisions each day, choices that strengthen your influence and help you lead more effectively.

At our company the first two words every new team member learns are "**It depends.**" Any leadership style can work. And sometimes that same leadership *won't* work. *It depends on the situation.* Over the years the world and the workplace have evolved, but the core principles of effective leadership haven't. There will always be a task to accomplish, a person (even if assisted) responsible for it, and a leader guiding the process. This book will help you recognize those moments for what they are—opportunities to adapt your approach, match what your people need, and lead with greater clarity, confidence, and impact.

The Power of Influence

You're a leader. Yes, *you*. Whether you have a formal title, a corner office, direct reports—or none of the above—you influence people every single day. That means every day, you're leading.

At work you influence your boss, teammates, clients, and customers. In your personal life, you influence your spouse, children, parents, and friends. Leadership isn't limited to a role or position; it's woven into how you show up in every arena of your life and how you respond to the moments in front of you.

Leadership is also everywhere—on sports fields and debate stages, in classrooms and community projects, in mentoring conversations and everyday parenting. Leaders inspire volunteers, rally teams, steward resources, and shape the next generation. They build momentum, remove barriers, and open doors for others. It's impossible to imagine a world without it.

> ❝ *Leadership is influence.*

And because leadership shows up in so many forms, we define it simply: **Leadership is influence.** Anytime you seek to influence the behavior of another person or group, you're leading. Your words, your presence, your choices, and your actions all carry weight. When used intentionally, that influence drives clarity, confidence, engagement, and results.

That's why leadership is worth learning. It's worth practicing. It's worth doing well. Because the better you understand how influence works, the more equipped you are to create environments where others can contribute, grow, and thrive.

What Great Leaders Do

If leadership is influence, then a natural next question is, *Why are some leaders better at influencing than others?* To answer this question, we invite you to consider your own experiences on the *receiving* end of leadership.

Think back to a time when you felt stuck and didn't know how to move forward, when you looked to your leader for help but got nothing actionable in return. Perhaps this stirs memories of the worst boss you ever had. How did this person's actions—or *inactions*—affect you? Many leaders describe feeling stressed, demotivated, disrespected, or even demeaned by leaders in their past. Others share that their boss's leadership damaged their work, their confidence, or even their careers.

If you've experienced bad leadership, you've learned a few lessons about what *not* to do. And it begins to illuminate the answer to that question about what leads to effective influence.

Now think about the best boss you've ever had. What did they do? What were they like? Did they make it enjoyable to come to work? Did they guide, support, encourage, and empower you? People often describe their best leaders as positive, inspiring, and deeply trustworthy—people who helped them navigate challenges, unlock potential they didn't know they had, and grow into the best versions of themselves. Great leadership is energizing, motivating, supportive, and empowering.

After studying thousands of effective leaders, we've found clear patterns. The best leaders meet the needs of both the individual and the situation. They connect people to a shared vision and the future direction of the team or organization. They create environments where people know what's expected, where to turn for help, and how to contribute meaningfully. In these environments innovation and collaboration thrive, and people feel part of something bigger than themselves. But effective leadership doesn't happen by accident. It requires commitment, intentionality, and the daily choice to grow and get better.

Positive Leadership Traits

Leaders who adapt well, build engagement, and consistently deliver results tend to share these traits:

Purpose-driven: They align vision, strategy, and execution.

Self-aware: They understand how emotions and behaviors influence others.

Trustworthy: They communicate honestly and follow through on commitments.

People-centric: They support others' growth, needs, and well-being.

Humble: They seek feedback and own mistakes.

Effective communicators: They listen well and build strong connections.

Learning agility: They stretch, adapt, and learn from experience.

Respectful and inclusive: They create safety, fairness, and belonging.

As you strengthen your leadership, focus on developing these traits; they'll make you a better leader!

Leadership Is Measured by Impact

Leadership isn't just about good intentions or creating a positive atmosphere. Ultimately, leaders are measured by their impact; and that impact shows up in three interconnected ways.

- **Success:** Are you and your team delivering consistent results and making steady progress? Or are you falling short and struggling with inconsistency?
- **Engagement:** Do people enjoy the work and feel challenged, supported, and encouraged to grow? Or are they disengaged, simply going through the motions, and missing opportunities to contribute?
- **Retention:** Are your best people staying, developing, and thriving? Or are they looking for opportunities elsewhere while your lowest performers settle in for the long haul?

For years organizations focused almost entirely on productivity metrics when evaluating leaders. But that's changing, and with good reason. Employee engagement is at a historic low. According to Gallup, only about 31 percent of workers are engaged, while fewer than half clearly understand what's expected of them.[1] The result? Most employees do what they're told and little more, costing the global economy an estimated $8.8 trillion annually.

Leaders who can regain even a fraction of that lost value are critical. Your role as a leader is to balance results and relationships, to drive productivity while also fostering engagement. The great news is that engagement fuels performance, which, in turn, drives productivity. It also strengthens loyalty, which means your top talent stays where they belong—on your team.

At The Center for Leadership Studies (CLS), we've studied exceptional leaders for decades. While the best certainly achieve success, they ensure the *longevity* of that success by consistently returning their focus to engagement. They create environments where people enjoy their work, feel challenged, keep learning and growing, and deliver outstanding results. These leaders build strong, connected teams—and they keep winning.

Leadership Is Multidirectional

Many of us think of leadership as something tied to hierarchy—a manager, executive, general, or parent. But if leadership is simply *influence*, then it isn't confined to titles or org charts. You influence others, and others influence you, all the time.

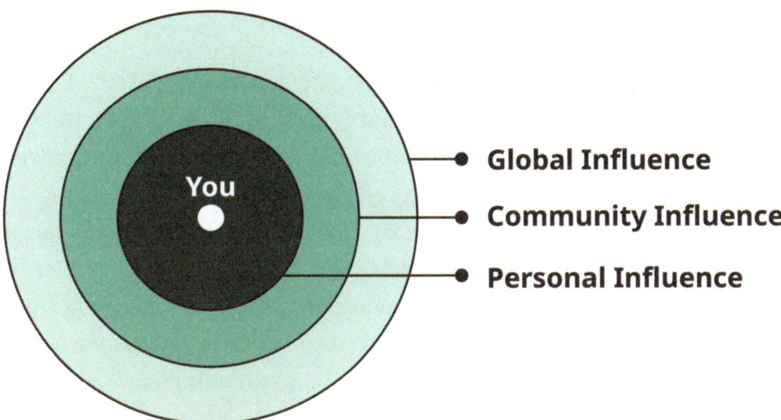

You'll see on this influence graphic that your sphere of influence includes your customers, boss, peers, and direct reports. Influence can move in many directions. And to get things done in today's world, you'll need to influence people you don't have formal authority over (and, of course, some that you do). Influence moves in three different directions: top-down, bottom-up, and peer-to-peer. Let's unpack these levels.

Traditional (Top-Down) Leadership

Traditional leadership occurs when influence flows from a formal position of power. The boss establishes priorities, defines success, and provides clear, objective feedback.

Many people first encounter the Situational Leadership® Model in this context—when organizations invest in developing managers to drive productivity more effectively. But today's expectations have evolved. Just because leadership is top-down doesn't mean the leader's voice is the only one that carries weight. Leaders are required to keep multiple factors in balance to be effective. That balance requires adaptability, and the Situational Leadership® Model helps leaders do exactly that—by equipping them to meet each follower where they are.

Follower-Driven (Bottom-Up) Leadership

Leadership is a two-way street. It's most effective when both the leader and follower are equally invested in a shared goal and aligned in how they pursue it. In this dynamic followers also have significant power to influence the leader—what we call "leading up."

This happens in two key ways. First, followers can use the language of the Situational Leadership® Model to describe their current state and ask for what they need: more direction, more support, or additional resources. As the performer, you understand your performance needs better than anyone else. Communicating those needs clearly, without judgment, helps leaders respond effectively.

Second, followers can lead up even without formal authority. If your leader gives direction that seems off-track, they're likely not trying to make your job harder; they just might not see what you see. Starting a respectful, solution-focused conversation allows you to share your perspective, suggest alternatives, and explain your reasoning.

Peer-to-Peer (Lateral) Leadership

Peer leadership has become essential these days with cross-functional teams, project groups, and task forces becoming the norm. In these environments no one holds formal authority, but everyone's expected to lead.

Defining who leads and who follows can feel tricky in these situations, but it ultimately comes down to responsibility. If you're accountable for the task, you're the leader, regardless of titles or hierarchy. Leadership simply takes a different form. You're still responsible for results, engagement, and collaboration. That means staying attuned to what the situation requires, understanding what each person needs to succeed, and adjusting your approach to keep the work moving and the team aligned.

As you continue through this book, consider how you can use the Situational Leadership® Model with your peers.

Developing Leaders

A recent global survey identified leadership development as one of the greatest challenges of the twenty-first century. For many organizations a weak leadership pipeline poses the biggest threat to their future. Companies everywhere are searching for effective leaders and recognizing that strong leadership is a true strategic asset. The companies that consistently lead their industries have one thing in common: They prioritize leadership. They see it as a core part of their competitive advantage and foster cultures that intentionally develop leaders at every level.

Power: The Fuel of Influence

You've seen that leadership isn't defined by title and that influence flows in every direction. But influence doesn't happen on its own. It needs fuel.

If leadership is influence, then what enables that influence to actually take place?

The answer is power.

Leadership is driven by power. And power is simply the potential to influence. The more power a leader has, the more effective they'll be as an influencer across all levels of an organization.

Imagine you're standing in a pitch-black room holding a flashlight. If the batteries are working, you press a button, light fills the space, and you can see where you're going. But if the batteries are dead, it doesn't matter how many times you click that button—you'll still be standing in the dark.

 *Power is the battery of leadership.*

Power is the battery of leadership. It's what allows you to "turn on your leadership light" and influence effectively. Power isn't optional when it comes to the Situational Leadership® Model. You can do everything right—identify the task, accurately assess a follower's Performance Readiness®, and choose the correct leadership style—but if you lack the power to drive that style, your attempt to influence will fall short. You simply cannot lead effectively without power.

To understand how power fuels influence, it helps to take a brief look at where our modern understanding of power began and how it's evolved over time.

A Brief History of Power

In full recognition of the fact that we live in the present, with an eye on the future, at CLS we freely admit to having an ongoing fascination with (and appreciation for) the past. We learn from history. We learn not only where our model comes from but how and why it integrates with and anchors to other core, common, and critical leadership concepts you see today. And you simply cannot talk intelligently about leadership without first understanding organizational power. So with those thoughts in mind, here's an abbreviated review.

For centuries researchers and practitioners have studied the relationship between leadership and power—a thread often traced back to Niccolò Machiavelli, an adviser to princes in 1500s Italy. His "clients" needed to compel their soldiers to enter battle again and again under extremely dangerous conditions. In that context Machiavelli asked a foundational question: *Is it better for a leader to be loved or feared?*

(In other words: *Would armies risk their lives because they loved their prince—or because they feared him?*)

He concluded that while both were desirable, if a leader had to choose, fear was more reliable. When lives were on the line, affection alone wasn't enough; princes who were feared were more effective at leading armies than those who weren't.

Centuries later sociologist Amitai Etzioni revisited this same question in a modern context: *If businesses were in a commercial war with competitors, why would employees follow their bosses into "battle"?* Studying large organizations in the 1960s, he reframed Machiavelli's ideas into two broad categories of power: position power (rooted in authority) and personal power (rooted in trust and identification). Even in a corporate setting, Etzioni's conclusion echoed Machiavelli's: Position power tended to be the more effective source of influence.

Soon afterward American social psychologists John R. P. French and Bertram Raven expanded Etzioni's work by identifying more distinct forms within those two buckets. Their goal was to clarify what specifically constituted position power versus personal power, and their research became a foundational taxonomy for understanding how leaders exert influence.

In the 1980s Dr. Hersey and Dr. Walt Natemeyer expanded the research by adding a seventh base of power—connection power. With that addition leaders now draw from seven distinct sources of influence: legitimate, reward, coercive, expert, referent, information, and connection. This evolution helped shape modern thinking about power and continues to inform how we understand a leader's potential to influence today.

The Seven Bases of Power

These are the seven bases of power identified through decades of leadership research. Each describes a different source of influence that potential leaders can draw from.

Legitimate Power: Based on the formal authority a leader has been given in the organization, including decision-making rights and role expectations.

Coercive Power: Based on the ability to administer sanctions or negative consequences (e.g., a police officer issuing a ticket).

Reward Power: Based on the leader's ability to distribute formal rewards such as raises, promotions, or recognition.

Expert Power: Based on the leader's relevant knowledge, credentials, experience, or technical expertise.

Referent Power: Based on the trust, respect, and credibility a leader earns through consistent investment in relationships and behavior over time.

Information Power: Added shortly after French and Raven's original research, this power comes from having access to valuable information (e.g., an executive assistant with access to the organization's strategic plans).

Connection Power: Based on the leader's relationships with key individuals in or beyond the organization and the access those relationships provide.

The Three Modern Bases of Power

Over time CLS revisited Hersey's work on power. By surveying how employees across a variety of industries, organization sizes, and generations responded to the existing seven power bases, they refined the most effective forms of power into three modern categories that describe how leaders influence today: legitimate power, expert power, and referent power.

Legitimate Power

Legitimate power stems from a leader's formal role within an organization. It reflects the authority to make decisions, establish priorities, and set expectations. When used well, legitimate power provides clarity and direction. When avoided or misused (like when leaders fail to make decisions or hold people accountable), it weakens the team as much as good leadership can strengthen it. Legitimate power also includes the authority to reward and sanction, reinforcing a leader's ability to set expectations and guide performance.

Expert Power

Expert power is influence rooted in knowledge or skill. It includes technical expertise, real-world experience, and information power, such as the ability to navigate systems, access needed details, and help others do the same. Leaders don't need to be the smartest person in the room; they simply need relevant knowledge or perspective that earns respect.

Referent Power

Referent power is influence based on trust. It's built through honesty, fairness, consistency, and genuine care for others. Unlike legitimate power, trust isn't something a leader can demand; followers choose how much they'll share, how openly they'll communicate, and how invested they'll be. We like to say that referent power takes a long time to earn and no time to burn—meaning, it can be lost quickly if leaders aren't careful. When it's strong, it becomes especially important during seasons of change or uncertainty.

You don't need all three sources of power in every situation to lead effectively. Understanding these three sources of power helps you see where your influence comes from and how to strengthen it. Legitimate power gives you authority to set direction. Expert power earns respect through knowledge and experience. Referent power builds trust and creates the relationships that sustain performance through change. When you know which forms of power you hold—and which ones you need to develop—you can more accurately assess your capability to effectively influence.

Now let's look at what these power bases look like in real life by exploring how one leader used all three to guide his team through a moment of deep uncertainty.

Power and Influence in Motion

A few years ago, we were brought in to coach the leadership team of a pharmaceutical company. They had recently lost their CEO—the highly visible leader of the organization—because of an ethics issue, and the team was devastated. Organizational trust was fractured.

One of the leaders, a director named Joshua, had been leading a large research department for ten years. Now he was responsible for guiding his people through the crisis, even as he struggled himself.

It would be no exaggeration to say the company was in chaos. No one knew what to do next. Although Joshua had been an engaged, committed, highly capable leader, he was shaken. He no longer felt confident, committed, or motivated. In fact, he was considering leaving the company altogether and was in the process of updating his résumé accordingly.

We had a highly memorable in-person meeting with Joshua at the height of all this drama. We began by asking him a series of questions designed to help him think through his situation and decide whether he wanted to stay and respond or move on. The questions were as follows:

- What's your number one concern?
- What can you do to address that concern?
- What decisions need to be made now, and what can wait?

We could see right away that these simple questions struck a nerve. Joshua spoke at least 90 percent of the time during that initial session, venting his frustrations at length. We listened, acknowledged the challenges, and offered empathy, but not advice.

Over time he talked himself into staying: "I care about this mission. I'm passionate about the people on this team, and I don't want to walk away from the work we've done. I've thought about it, and I think I know what we need to do."

We could feel the shift. He was ready to step up and lead.

He created a plan to weather the storm, and he began by engaging his team much the same way we had engaged him. He asked them whether they wanted to stay and be part of the solution. Then together, they updated their plan, aligned on priorities, and established how they'd monitor progress.

He also verbally acknowledged how disruptive the crisis had been and worked intentionally to help people process what they were experiencing. He encouraged them at every opportunity. And while other departments lost key contributors, Joshua's team didn't. His people stayed, and they continued meaningful research and development that might one day save lives.

Joshua's leadership kept his team together. In short he influenced them effectively. Why? Because his team believed he

- knew what he was talking about (expert power),
- deserved to be heard (legitimate power), and
- had their best interests in mind (referent power).

Joshua held formal authority, but more importantly, he had earned credibility and trust, and he leveraged all three sources of power when he needed them most.

He had

- set high standards;
- held people accountable, including himself;
- built strong working relationships; and
- proven he was fair, honest, and dependable.

So when disruption hit, his team looked to him and followed him.

Trust Reigns

Joshua's story illustrates an important truth: While authority and expertise play a big role, trust is what ultimately keeps people aligned, committed, and willing to follow through uncertainty. And let's be honest; uncertainty is becoming more the norm.

That pattern isn't just anecdotal; it's reinforced by the broader research behind those findings. In the power studies conducted by CLS, both leaders and followers evaluated how the seven bases showed up in real workplace situations. Both groups agreed that every base of power still works today. Each was rated at least 65 percent effective in explaining why people complied with their manager's attempts to influence.

But there was a meaningful difference in how leaders and followers viewed which bases were most key. Leaders assumed that legitimate power (authority, position, title) was their strongest source of influence. Followers disagreed. They responded more strongly to referent power (trust, respect, relationship) and expert power (credible knowledge and experience).

In other words people follow leaders they believe are trustworthy and knowledgeable—exactly what Joshua's team saw in him.

> **“** *People follow leaders they believe are trustworthy and knowledgeable.*

This gap says a lot about how power functions today. The modern workforce is less impressed by positional authority and more responsive to leaders they believe are honest, fair, competent, and genuinely invested in their best interests. This will probably only become even more noticeable as organizations flatten and legitimate power becomes less common. For many, especially Gen Z, trust has become the currency of work. And that trust (or lack thereof) shapes nearly every decision: whether people are honest with you, bring their best effort, share what's really going on, or stay through difficult seasons.

The funny thing about trust is that it's not something a leader can demand. It's earned over time, through consistent behavior, fairness, honesty, and care. But investing that time means expanding your impact—*exponentially*. When trust rises, conversations are more candid, collaboration strengthens, and engagement and retention climb. In other words, while legitimate, expert, and referent power all have their place, trust reigns.

When you're influencing a peer, you rarely have legitimate power to rely on. Instead, you draw primarily on referent power (trust) and expert power (credibility). That means how you initiate the conversation is crucial, especially when you're offering guidance or direction.

You might begin by sharing your own experience.

"I ran into this same challenge; can I share what helped me?"

or

"Let's walk through a few options. I can show you what I tried."

From there, offer "safe outs" so the other person can guide the conversation rather than feeling pressured.

"How does that approach land for you?"

"Do you think that would work in your situation?"

When you listen well, show empathy, and let peers talk through their scenario in their own words, trust grows. You also open the door for them to ask for help and be more transparent about obstacles getting in the way.

Leadership Is Learned

When it comes to Situational Leadership®, you can follow the model perfectly, but if you don't have sufficient legitimate, expert, and referent power, your attempt to influence will fall short. Although power isn't specifically called out in the Situational Leadership® Model, leadership and power have always been two sides of the same coin.

You don't "do" power; you do leadership. But your ability to lead effectively is driven by the power you have with others. Leaders can easily make the mistake of skipping the power consideration and jumping right into influencing, only to find that others don't respond to their attempts. The success of your leadership—and the engagement of the people doing the work—is directly tied to the influence potential (a.k.a. power) you bring to each situation.

The way we leverage power bases differs depending on the situation. For example, when a skilled employee suddenly loses confidence in their ability to do what they're best at, a leader has to lean on referent power to identify the root cause of this shift and rebuild their confidence. On the other hand, when a team member is intimidated by a change initiative and refuses to engage in the related training, a leader might need to flex their legitimate power to create clear expectations, or perhaps use expert power to explain in detail why the change is necessary.

While we've highlighted some of the traits and tendencies of effective leaders, it's important to remember that leadership isn't just personality, potential, or position—it's a skill. There's long been debate over whether leaders are born or made. And while some people may have a natural inclination to influence others, the evidence is clear: Leadership can be developed. In fact, it's one of the most important skills you *should* develop. And like any skill, it grows through practice and persistence. Studying leadership concepts is valuable, but true growth happens when you apply what you've learned, reflect on the outcome, and keep refining your approach.

After you learn the Situational Leadership® Model, improvement comes through consistent practice—working with people over time, paying attention to what works and what doesn't, and becoming increasingly self-aware. Great leaders seek feedback, adapt their approach, and stay intentional about how they communicate and influence. Unlike elite athletes or performers, there's no limit to how many world-class leaders the world can hold. You can become one of them. It's simply a matter of committing to the process and continually getting better.

Chapter 1 Review

- Leadership is influence, and influence shows up *everywhere*, regardless of title or position.
- Effective leadership is measured through success, engagement, and retention.
- Influence flows in all directions: top-down, bottom-up, and peer-to-peer.
- Power is the fuel of influence; without it, even the right leadership approach won't land.
- Modern research highlights three core power bases that drive today's influence: legitimate, expert, and referent power.
- Followers respond most strongly to referent and expert power; trust and credibility carry more weight than authority alone.
- Trust amplifies every form of power and is essential for commitment, honesty, and long-term performance.
- Leadership is a skill you can hone. With awareness, practice, and feedback, anyone can strengthen their influence.

Reflect and Apply

Before you move on, take a moment to reflect on how this chapter applies to your leadership today.

1. Think of the best or worst leader you've experienced. What forms of power did they rely on most, and how did it affect you?
2. Where is your influence most active right now—top-down, bottom-up, or peer-to-peer?
3. What's one concrete way you can strengthen your referent power with someone you lead this week?

Building the Model

*Introducing Performance Readiness®
and Leadership Styles*

Our team recently worked with a team specializing in public policy, and one of their senior leaders, Liam, shared his frustration right away. "This new generation is driving me nuts," he said. "We get on Zoom calls with high-level government officials, and they're showing up in T-shirts and ball caps. They have their PhDs, but they're so unprofessional. It's maddening."

We asked a few more questions. "Besides the T-shirts, what other behaviors are you seeing that cause problems?"

"Well," he sighed, "they get on calls with major funders or government partners and talk like they're chatting with friends. They don't do their homework to understand who's on the other side of the screen. And when they send emails, it's like they're sending text messages—with emojis and slang. But I can't fire them all, or I'll be shorthanded."

We nodded. "That sounds really frustrating. What if we treat professionalism as the task your people need to accomplish?"

"Huh?" he said, leaning back. "Is professionalism really something you can develop in people? How would I do that?"

We started listing possibilities. "It sounds like professionalism isn't just one thing in your organization. It's several skills. Polished written communication. Knowing how to show up for a call. Doing the right research. Communicating appropriately with partners." We wrote each one on the whiteboard. "If we treat each as its own task, we can figure out how to lead your people in developing them."

Liam nodded slowly. "They're not all at the same level, that's for sure. Jasmine shows up looking polished most of the time, and Daniel writes a solid email." Together, we evaluated where each person was strongest and where they needed support and growth.

Finally, Liam sat back with a smile on his face. "Okay. Obviously I'll need to lead differently in each of these situations. Walk me through how that works."

When we visited a few weeks later, Liam was excited to report on his team's progress. "You know what? A lot of this was an easy fix," he told us. "I just hadn't had a direct conversation. Two people were grateful for the feedback and turned things around right away. I let one person go, and we moved another into a non-client-facing role. Honestly, I think half the problem was me. I hadn't communicated my expectations or coached them. I just got frustrated. Once I realized they could develop, everything changed."

Liam's experience is common. Some leadership challenges feel overwhelming and impossible to solve—until you look at them through a simple lens: how ready each person is to do what's being asked of them. A couple of Liam's team members were more than willing to make some changes and get to work. The other two were clearly in different places. Had he treated all four the same way, he likely would have stayed frustrated and seen little improvement.

Instead, by considering where each person was at, he could respond differently. Some needed clear direction. Others needed support and coaching. One needed to be reassigned. Matching his approach to what each person needed in that moment made all the difference.

When you pay attention to a person's readiness—what we'll unpack in this chapter—the path forward becomes clearer. And once you understand where someone is, you can respond in a way that supports their growth and performance. That's the foundation of the Situational Leadership® Model: Different people require different kinds of leadership depending on their readiness for a specific task.

Diagnosing Performance Readiness®

What do we mean by "readiness"?

In the Situational Leadership® Model, readiness refers to a person's current ability and willingness to do what's being asked of them. It reflects where someone is right now, not who they are overall.

> ❝ *At the heart of this model is a focus on others.*

Readiness is always tied to a specific task. A person isn't simply "ready" or "not ready" in general; they're ready for a particular responsibility. In other words the task drives *everything*. Someone may be confident and skilled in one area and unsure in another. Before you can assess readiness or decide how to lead, you must have a shared understanding of what success looks like for that task. Once the task is clear, the question becomes, "Is this person able and willing to perform it?" (More on identifying the task in chapter 5.)

At the heart of this model is a focus on others, on understanding what your follower needs to perform successfully. We call this:

Performance Readiness®
The degree of demonstrated ability and willingness to perform a specific task.

To understand our own and others' Performance Readiness®, we'll look at two key factors relative to the task.

Ability
The knowledge, experience, and skill an individual demonstrates for a particular task

Willingness
The confidence, commitment, and motivation an individual brings to performing it

Ability Versus Capability

It's common to confuse ability with capability or potential. The Situational Leadership® Model doesn't measure what someone *could* do someday. It's about what they're demonstrating *right now*. Ability reflects current performance—not tomorrow, not next week, and not six months ago.

If you're unsure whether someone is truly able or simply capable, ask yourself, *Are they currently performing the task at a sustained, acceptable level? And if they continued performing this way, would you be satisfied?*

Willingness

Willingness doesn't just describe attitude; it reflects confidence, commitment, and motivation for the task at hand. A follower may be temporarily "unwilling" because they're discouraged, distracted, or overwhelmed. That unwillingness might be demonstrated through the following:

- A high performer struggling with self-doubt
- A caregiver balancing heavy personal responsibilities
- A team member who's overcommitted
- A professional facing public pressure or fear of failure

The following are four combinations of demonstrated ability and willingness that determine a person's Performance Readiness® Level for a particular task:

- **R1: Unable and Insecure or Unwilling**
  A low level of readiness. The person lacks the skill to perform the task and lacks either the confidence or motivation to take it on.

- **R2: Unable but Confident or Willing**
  A low to moderate level of readiness. The person is eager to learn and motivated to perform but hasn't yet demonstrated the required skill. They're willing, just not yet able.

- **R3: Able but Insecure or Unwilling**
  A moderate to high level of readiness. The person has the skill to perform but is struggling with either confidence or motivation. They're able to perform, but they're also hesitant, uncertain, or disengaged.

- **R4: Able and Confident and Willing**
  A high level of readiness. The person can consistently perform the task to standard and brings the confidence, commitment, and motivation to do so independently.

Now let's see how these levels play out in real life. For this next section, put yourself in the shoes of the follower.

R1

Low Performance Readiness®

R1
Unable and Insecure or Unwilling
Behavioral Indicators
Apprehensive
Avoiding
Defensiveness
Discomfort
No progress
Procrastinating
Questioning task

You've been assigned a task you've never done before. You're surprised and intimidated, unsure where to start or even how to ask for help. You don't want to let your boss or your teammates down. In other words you're insecure and unable to do this task.

LEADERSHIP RESPONSE:

In this situation you need a boss who takes control—someone who directs you, tells you exactly what to do and how to do it, checks in often, provides feedback, and recognizes progress as you build confidence.

R2

Unable but Confident or Willing

Behavioral Indicators

Eager to learn

Enthusiastic

Interested

Receptive to input

Requires context

Seeks clarity

Self-assured

R2

Low to Moderate Performance Readiness®

You're given a completely new task. You've never done this before, but you're eager to dive in and get started. You're sure no one will work harder, progress quicker, or produce more than you. What you lack in experience, you'll make up for in effort. In other words you're unable but willing.

LEADERSHIP RESPONSE:

When enthusiasm is high but skill is low, the best boss provides structure and coaching while recognizing and applauding enthusiasm. They explain the *why* behind the work, encourage your progress, and keep your motivation aligned with learning.

R3

Moderate to High Performance Readiness®

R3
Able but Insecure or Unwilling
Behavioral Indicators Anxious Discomfort Frustrated Hesitant Resistant Seeks reinforcement Questions ability

You've worked alongside your boss on this task for a while and feel comfortable in that partnership. Then your boss asks you to take the lead. You know what to do and how to do it but feel uncomfortable if your boss isn't going to be there with you. In other words you're able but insecure.

LEADERSHIP RESPONSE:

When ability is strong but insecurity is holding you back, you need a boss who listens to your concerns and helps build your confidence. They acknowledge your experience and skill and assure you that, if problems arise, you have what it takes to handle them. They're passing ownership to you—a critical part of achieving full mastery over a task.

R4
Able and Confident and Willing
Behavioral Indicators Consistent performance Demonstrates expertise Self-reliant Shares progress Operates efficiently Takes initiative Works autonomously

R4

High Performance Readiness®

You've been doing this task for a while now, and some might say you've even mastered it. Few others can operate at your same level of skill and experience, and that makes you proud. In other words you're able and willing.

LEADERSHIP RESPONSE:

When you're performing at this level, you need autonomy. The best boss gives you space to perform while remaining available when and if you need support. They recognize your track record of performance and trust you to do your own work.

As you read those examples, you may recognize moments from your own career—times when you needed more direction, encouragement, or independence. That's the beauty of this model—it helps you see leadership from both sides. You can understand what you need when being led and what others need when looking to you.

Each of the scenarios you just explored shows a follower at one point on the Performance Readiness® continuum. That readiness reflects current ability and willingness for a specific task.

For example, a single salesperson might be

- R4 for customer interactions,
- R1 for new administrative systems,
- R3 for presenting quarterly reports, and
- R2 for learning a new product line.

The same person can occupy all four readiness levels, depending on the task. That's why leaders have to stay alert and adaptable rather than typecasting people as "high" or "low" performers.

That said, there's an important nuance to keep in mind here too. Developing readiness isn't a linear process or a rigid progression. People don't move neatly from R1 to R4 like climbing a ladder. Growth is dynamic. Someone might skip levels, regress, or fluctuate depending on confidence, circumstances, or even external stressors. Ebbs and flows of confidence and willingness during these transitions are normal— they're part of what makes leadership a relationship, not a formula.

Performance Readiness®

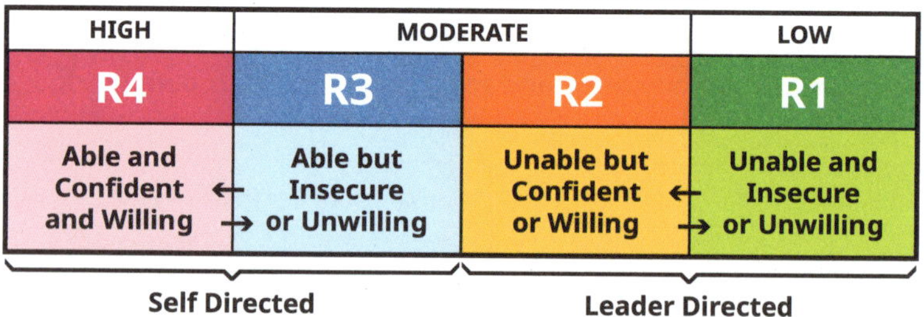

An Objective Model

One reason the Situational Leadership® Model is so effective across the globe is that it's objective. It's guided by facts, not emotions, preferences, or favoritism. That objectivity builds trust and consistency and ensures that effort and performance are recognized fairly.

A leader's response always depends on two things: the situation and the follower's demonstrated ability and willingness for the task. The good news is that these factors aren't guesswork; they're observable. You should be able to clearly articulate the cues that informed your Performance Readiness® diagnosis and share concrete examples to confirm alignment with the follower. Once you know how to read those cues, you can choose the right leadership style in almost any circumstance.

Now let's put these readiness levels into the larger framework to visualize how leadership and Performance Readiness® connect.

Task and Relationship Behaviors

When you look at the Situational Leadership® Model, you'll notice that the Performance Readiness® continuum forms its foundation. This reflects the idea that leadership begins with the needs of the follower for a specific task, based on a specific situation.

The model builds on what you've just learned about ability and willingness, showing how those readiness levels connect directly to leadership behavior. In other words once you've identified where someone falls on the readiness continuum, you can determine the type of leadership they need from you. We previewed some of those responses in the scenarios above; now we'll take a closer look at what each one involves.

With readiness in place, we move to the top half of the model—leadership styles. The four boxes you see represent four styles, each

Situational Leadership®
Influence Behaviors

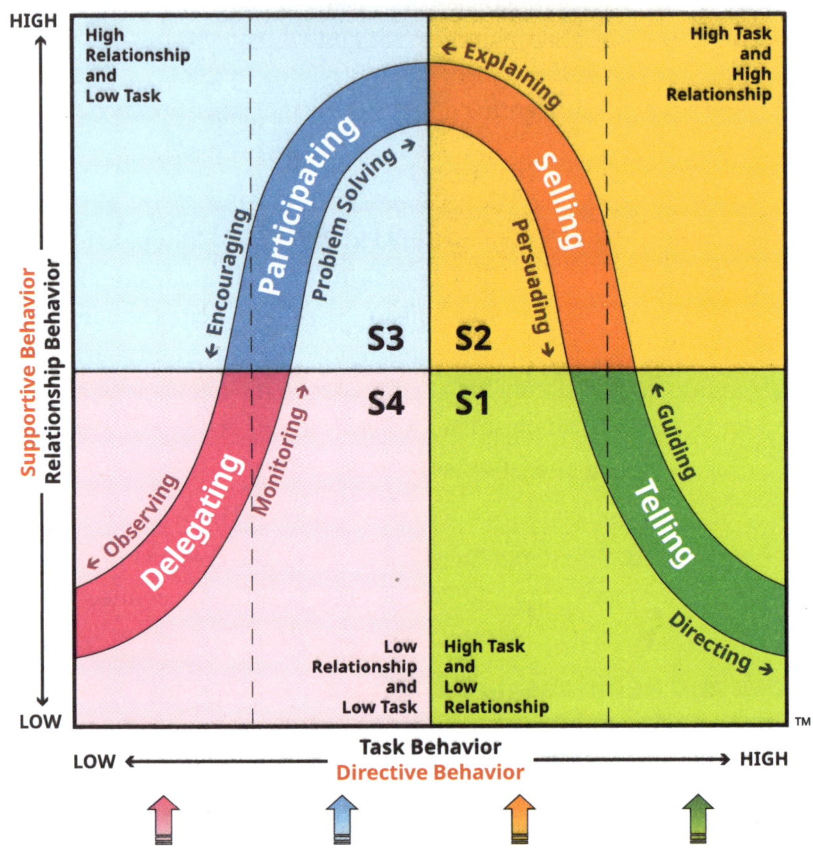

Performance Readiness®

HIGH	MODERATE		LOW
R4	**R3**	**R2**	**R1**
Able and Confident and Willing ←	Able but Insecure or Unwilling →	Unable but Confident or Willing ←	Unable and Insecure or Unwilling →

Self Directed   **Leader Directed**

Situational Leadership® and Performance Readiness® are trademarks of Leadership Studies, Inc.
Copyright © 2022 Leadership Studies, Inc. All rights reserved.

combining two core behaviors: task behavior and relationship behavior. A leader can use high or low amounts of each.

Notice the y- and x-axes, labeled "Relationship Behavior" and "Task Behavior." Each style is a different combination of these two types of behaviors, ranging from low to high on either axis.

Task Behavior (X-Axis)

Task behavior,
or directive behavior, is the extent to which a leader defines roles and structures activities. This is where you

- *define outcomes and goals,*
- *establish timelines and priorities, and*
- *set standards and monitor performance.*

Leaders on the right side of the model demonstrate higher amounts of task behavior; they provide clear direction and structure, which means the leadership approach is more leader-directed. Leaders on the left side demonstrate lower amounts of task behavior; they give people more autonomy in how work gets done, making the approach increasingly more self- or follower-directed.

Relationship Behavior (Y-Axis)

Relationship behavior,
or supportive behavior, focuses on how a leader engages in two-way communication and listening. This is where you

- *encourage dialogue and invite feedback,*
- *listen actively and facilitate collaboration, and*
- *offer support, reassurance, and recognition.*

Leaders using S2 or S3 rely on higher amounts of relationship behavior, focusing heavily on communication and support. Those using S1 or S4 use lower amounts of relationship behavior (for very different reasons).

It's worth noting that with relationship behavior, low doesn't mean *zero*. The ends of the curve make this clear: There's never a moment when a leader provides no relationship behavior. Every style includes at least some support; it's the amount that changes from style to style.

Together, these two axes—task behavior on the x-axis and relationship behavior on the y-axis—form the four leadership styles. The power of Situational Leadership® lies in recognizing that *no single style is best*. The most effective influence approach depends on what your follower needs to perform the task successfully.

Influence Behaviors

Above the bell curve of the Situational Leadership® Model is the phrase "Influence Behaviors." Earlier, we defined leadership as influence, so it's only fitting that the four leadership styles represent influence behaviors. These are the actions a leader uses to attempt to influence others. In the model they specifically describe how a leader attempts to influence performers as they develop along the Performance Readiness® continuum shown below the bell curve.

The Four Leadership Styles

Now that you understand task and relationship behaviors, we can look at how they combine in different ways to form four distinct leadership styles. Don't worry about memorizing each one yet; we'll work with them in greater depth in chapter 7. For now we're just getting familiar with the model.

Style 1 (S1): Telling, Directing, Guiding

S1
High Task and Low Relationship
Behavioral Indicators Convey decisions Define goals Establish milestones Give instructions Initiate movement Provide specifics

High Task, Low Relationship

Leader-directed: "I talk. I decide."

This leadership style provides clear, detailed direction with the goal of creating movement and getting the follower going. It's decisive and structured, ensuring clarity when ability and willingness are low.

Style 2 (S2): Selling, Persuading, Explaining

S2
High Task and High Relationship
Behavioral Indicators Confirm understanding Deliver feedback Encourage questions Explain why Provide details Reinforce improvements

High Task, High Relationship

Leader-directed: "We talk. I decide."

This approach leverages the follower's enthusiasm while building skill. The leader gives direction and structure but also explains and discusses the why behind the task.

S3
High Relationship and Low Task
Behavioral Indicators Build confidence Compliment performance Discuss apprehension Enable next steps Solicit input Synthesize concerns

High Relationship, Low Task

Self-directed: "We talk. You decide."

This style supports followers who have ability but need reassurance. The leader facilitates discussion, provides encouragement, and helps the follower step into ownership.

S4
Low Relationship and Low Task
Behavioral Indicators Encourage autonomy Eliminate barriers Entrust decision-making Remain accessible Resist overloading Track progress

Low Relationship, Low Task

Self-directed: "You decide. I trust you."

This approach empowers high-performing and confident followers to continue to master the task. The leader provides space and autonomy while remaining available if needed.

Each leadership style can always be personalized in a way that feels authentic to the leader. A top-down leader using S1 might communicate with a commanding tone—"telling." A peer-to-peer leader using the same style might approach it more collaboratively—"guiding." The core behaviors stay the same; the tone simply fits the context.

Remember, the right approach depends on your follower's ability and willingness for the task. To be effective, you'll need to diagnose your follower's readiness for that specific task, then match your leadership style accordingly. For example, a follower at R1 will need an S1 style. Both are labeled "1"—and both are green—indicating that they're a match.

Veering away from the corresponding number and color—such as using S3 when your follower is at R1 for a task—would indicate a mismatch. The mismatch is in color, yes, but more importantly it represents the wrong mix of influence behaviors for the situation.

You'll learn exactly how to match each leadership style to your follower's readiness level in later chapters. For now, recognize that effective leadership is about being flexible and intentional, knowing when to direct, when to coach, when to encourage, and when to step back.

What Followers Need Most

In a LinkedIn survey of two thousand professionals,[2] leadership expert Marshall Goldsmith asked, "What does your leader need to do better?"

Surprisingly, the top answer wasn't "Give more freedom." It was "Provide clearer direction."

The remaining responses were evenly divided among coaching, supporting, and delegating, essentially mirroring the four leadership styles. As Goldsmith quipped, "You're looking at the Situational Leadership® Model."

Empowerment isn't always what people need. As Goldsmith warned, "You take somebody with no motivation, no ability, and delegate—you have a disaster. And participation isn't always good either . . . get ten people in a room who know nothing, and you're just pooling ignorance."

The Groundwork for Great Leadership

You might already be experiencing some aha moments, recognizing times when your leadership style didn't quite fit the situation. That's one of the best parts of learning this model—it gives language to things you've felt intuitively but may not have been able to name.

And that's exactly where we'll eventually go—into how to use the model in real time to diagnose readiness and respond with the right style. We'll give you practical skills, tools, and examples to help you put all this into action. For now the most important takeaway is this: The Situational Leadership® Model marries two key components— readiness and leadership styles.

It's a people-centric model. It begins not with the leader's preference or personality but with the follower and with their ability and willingness to perform a specific task at a specific moment. Only then does the leader choose the approach that fits. All this is grounded in current, live, real-world dynamics, in how people really behave and what they actually need to be successful.

But before you start thinking we just woke up one day and invented this framework, let's pause. One of the reasons the Situational Leadership® Model has endured is because it's rooted in decades of leadership research. That has always been part of our DNA at CLS. We don't just coach leaders or facilitate workshops—we study leadership. And we've been doing so from the very start.

The two core components we've just introduced—readiness and leadership style—didn't originate with us. Their roots reach back to some of the earliest, most influential leadership studies ever conducted.

Over the next few chapters, we'll trace the most relevant aspects of that history, not as a nostalgic trip down memory lane but because this historical foundation is part of what makes the model so powerful. Understanding where these ideas came from, how they evolved, and why they remain universally relevant today gives you the context to apply the model confidently. It helps you see why each component exists and the evidence behind its legitimacy so you can adapt it to every situation with clarity and conviction.

In chapter 3, we'll begin with the origins of leadership styles and why early researchers focused on task and relationship behavior. Then in chapter 4, we'll explore the development of Performance Readiness® and how ability and willingness came to define follower needs. This is our origin story, and it's also why the model continues to resonate with leaders at every level and in every walk of life.

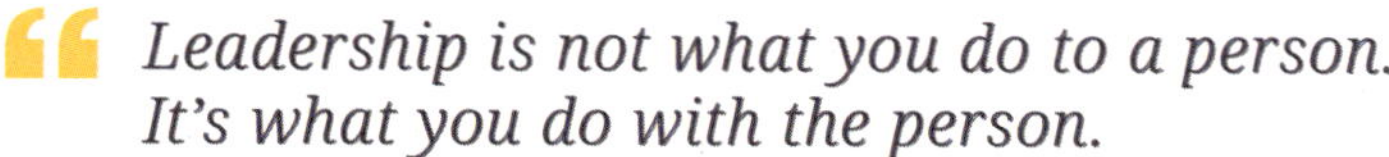

> *Leadership is not what you do to a person. It's what you do with the person.*
> —Dr. Paul Hersey

Chapter 2 Review

Here are the key takeaways from chapter 2:

- Everyone has a natural leadership style, but no single style works in every situation.
- The Situational Leadership® Model helps leaders assess what their people need for a specific task and adjust their approach accordingly.
- Readiness is always **task-specific**, not a judgment of someone's overall capability or potential.
- There are four Performance Readiness® Levels, representing someone's current ability and willingness to perform a specific task: R1, R2, R3, and R4.

- **Ability** reflects current performance, not potential (or *capability*), and **willingness** reflects confidence, commitment, and motivation for the task today.
- There are four leadership styles that align with a level of Performance Readiness®: S1, S2, S3, and S4.
- No style is "best." The most effective style is the one that fits the follower's readiness for the task.
- The model is objective and grounded in observable behavior, helping leaders and followers align with what's needed for success.

Reflect and Apply

Before you move on, take a moment to reflect on how this chapter applies to your leadership today.

1. Choose one task and one follower. Where would you place them on the Performance Readiness® continuum today?
2. What observations led you to that conclusion?
3. Where might you need to adjust your leadership approach to better match what the follower needs right now?

The Origins of Leadership Styles

*I never read any history books . . .
so I watch every historical documentary
on the edge of my seat.*
—Nate Bargatze, comedian

The Situational Leadership® Model is arguably the most scientifically informed leadership model ever developed. It was created by drawing on hundreds of studies in behavioral and organizational science over decades, and we've written about most of them in the book *Management of Organizational Behavior*.

But the book you're holding in your hands isn't a textbook (you're welcome), and it's not intended to be a survey course either. Instead, we ask you to walk with us through the most important milestones and debates that shaped the path to our modern understanding of what makes a Situational Leader (and we promise, it's fascinating).

We'll explore only the most significant studies that contributed to the Situational Leadership® framework. We'll discuss the history that makes those studies make sense, with an eye to the problems and changes each researcher was addressing. Most importantly, though, we'll look at all this through the lens of modern leadership: what makes a good leader, how leader behavior is related to (but also different from) predisposition or attitude, and how and why the model continues to provide critical guidance for today's most pressing problems.

Leadership has always evolved in response to change and in the pursuit of better performance and productivity. Today, AI is on the precipice of rewriting the rules of work; in just a few years, it's already shifted hiring practices and reshaped entire industries. No one quite knows what the future will look like, only that it'll bring historic change.

> **"** *Leadership has always evolved in response to change and in the pursuit of better performance and productivity.*

But the thing about historic change is that it's pretty common, *historically speaking*. Leaders have guided organizations through the rollout of personal computing, the rise of the internet, the adoption of smartphones, the transition to flexible work, and a global pandemic. Long before that, they navigated world-altering shifts and events such as electrification, the printing press, and the first powered flight. With every decade, every study, and every new challenge, leaders have refined their understanding of what effective leadership requires.

The more things change, the more we need leaders who can help people adapt to the world they now inhabit.

Our study begins with one of these world-changing eras: the Industrial Revolution. Before it, goods were produced in homes or small workshops, with skills passed down through apprenticeships. As industrialization accelerated, that way of working disappeared. Goods could now be manufactured more cheaply and efficiently in factories, prompting millions to leave rural farms—most untrained, unprepared, and overwhelmed by the unfamiliar environment. But they were ready to work! And they were ready to be led.

Before this shift, the only universally recognized organizations were the military, government, and the Catholic Church. "Leadership"—at least the distinction between good and bad leadership—wasn't really a concept. There were simply leaders—people granted authority. But factory work made it clear that this new kind of labor required a different approach. Good leaders inspired and protected workers; bad leaders harmed people and damaged equipment. Poor leadership meant illness, injury, death, lower productivity, and future workers unwilling to return. Good leadership wasn't just altruistic—it was essential.

What, then, made a good leader? What motivated workers? These were high-stakes questions. So began the systematic study of leadership—work that would, decades later, set the stage for our founder and the creation of the Situational Leadership® Model.

Behavioral and Organizational Science

Since the Situational Leadership® Model is grounded in both behavioral science and organizational science, it's helpful to define each.

Behavioral science studies human behavior to understand how people think, make decisions, and interact.

Organizational science examines how organizations function—their structures, processes, and the behaviors of people within them.

As you can see, there's significant overlap, especially when it comes to behavior in the workplace. Modern leaders draw on insights from these sciences to motivate teams, influence behavior, and design effective communication. By understanding behavior at a deeper level, leaders create environments that support performance, engagement, and change.

Taylor and Task Behavior

As the systematic study of leadership began, one of the first and most influential voices was Frederick Winslow Taylor, born in 1856. Educated in the Ivy League as a mechanical engineer, Taylor approached organizations the way an engineer approaches production, focusing on precision, efficiency, and control. Factory owners began hiring him as a third-party expert to diagnose problems and increase productivity. In that role he viewed organizations much like machinery and workers as the cogs that kept the system moving.

Taylor became one of the world's first management consultants, working with factories to increase production on assembly lines. He initiated time-and-motion studies to analyze work tasks, refined techniques and tools, and shared his observations with management. Productivity and efficiency increased, and Taylor's methods quickly spread.

This approach came to be known as scientific management, which assumed that organizations worked best when rationally planned. The leader should be autocratic, give clear directions and performance criteria, and enforce those criteria. Workers who excelled should receive incentive pay. Those who struggled should be held accountable. Processes should be studied and inefficiencies eliminated.

In Taylor's approach the leader made decisions, interpreted data, and told workers what to do, how to do it, and when it should be done. Training each worker in the "one best way" to do a job would lead to the greatest gains.

By 1910 scientific management had become famous worldwide as the answer to how leaders should lead and how organizations could maximize output. Taylor's work represents the beginning of modern leadership development, and his legacy is still visible today. Many modern performance systems—Six Sigma, Lean Manufacturing, and Lean Startup—are built on foundations he articulated: data, process, and the belief that tools and technique are just as essential as individual effort. His work is still cited in modern research, including studies of human performance, big data, and equity theory.

But even in his own day, Taylor drew criticism for treating workers like machines. Job satisfaction, motivation, and creativity played little role in his system. Labor unions pushed back, calling scientific management unnecessarily cold. And today, pure autocratic leadership is widely recognized as too limited; it often stifles initiative, flattens engagement, drains creativity, and drives talented people away.

Still, the style has its place. When we're new to a job, unclear about expectations, or facing an emergency that requires immediate action, we often want a leader who'll take charge. We actually saw a modern version of this during the COVID-19 era. Most of us had never worked from home or seriously ever thought about it. Suddenly, we all had to. People didn't know how to do it, and they were practically *screaming* for autocratic behavior—someone to step in, take charge, and tell them exactly what to do. For the most part, we got very little (because no one knew what to do!). We struggled our way through it, adapted as best we could, and eventually made it work.

Moments like these remind us that sometimes autocratic leadership is exactly what people need. But we've learned it's not a sustainable long-term approach. It's a style designed to create movement when people are new, unsure, or facing something unfamiliar. Taylor's work legitimized that kind of structure. But in his era, managers often abused it. They didn't "tell"; they yelled. They leaned on coercive power. That's part of why the style developed such a negative reputation.

When you look at the Situational Leadership® Model, it becomes clear how much of Taylor's thinking still echoes today. The task, or directive, axis closely mirrors the structure he championed in his early work—this is autocratic leadership. He gave the field its first vocabulary for studying how leaders define roles, structure work, and drive performance.

Next, the world would change again; this time not through prosperity but hardship. The Great Depression pushed society to question whether rational rules alone could get the most out of people. It wasn't enough. Workers needed more. And into this world stepped Elton Mayo.

Mayo and Relationship Behavior

Mayo was an industrial psychologist in the 1920s and 1930s, whose worldview was shaped early by his experience listening to Australian soldiers returning from World War I. Before anyone understood PTSD, he was thrust into the role of counseling disconsolate, disillusioned veterans—men stepping off ships with invisible wounds and no language to describe them. Psychologists such as Mayo were deployed by the government simply to listen, comfort, and help steady these men as they tried to reenter civilian life. Through that work, Mayo realized that people aren't machines, that decisions affect them, and that they need to be heard.

His contributions, like Taylor's, would prove to be timeless. But the spirit behind his early work was entirely different. In a time when hierarchies ruled and leadership relied almost entirely on legitimate power, Mayo was talking with workers, asking how they felt, inviting their suggestions, and treating them as humans with insight, not just cogs in a system. That alone was radical.

His most famous work took place at the Hawthorne Electric Plant outside Chicago, where he and his research team spent years studying workers. One group in particular was exclusively women who assembled relay switches. Part of Mayo's charter was to examine the effects of illumination on productivity. So his team cranked the lights up so high the women were sweating, and they noted that productivity went up. Then they dimmed the lights so low the women were working in near darkness, and productivity *still* went up. The results left the researchers baffled.

When they asked the workers why they'd picked up their pace, the answer was simple: Someone was paying attention to them. In the middle of the Great Depression, most of these women were underpaid and doing monotonous work, working in a factory instead of being home, doing what they had always done because they had to do it. But even then they wanted to matter! Any sign that someone noticed their effort or cared about their work pushed them to try a little harder. It was one of the earliest, clearest demonstrations that people respond to being seen—even in the most challenging circumstances.

The researchers then asked the women directly how productivity might improve even further. The workers offered suggestions, many of which, when implemented, worked. In other words the workers had valuable insights their leadership didn't. This was nothing short of astonishing at the time when plant operations were largely governed by the principles of scientific management.

From this research Mayo developed what became known as the human relations movement. He argued that alongside the formal structure of the workplace was an informal organization of people—real humans who needed purpose, connection, and care. When workers felt listened to and their ideas were valued, performance improved. When they felt ignored or devalued, performance dropped. (And it had nothing to do with lighting!)

In this new paradigm, the leader's job wasn't to dictate tasks but to actively involve workers in planning and execution. The leader should listen, engage, inspire, and occasionally guide. Their role was to facilitate and unlock success, not to *drive* it. This orientation represents the foundation of the relationship, or supportive, behavior axis in the Situational Leadership® Model.

The human relations movement went on to influence research in employee engagement, servant leadership, psychological safety, and inclusivity. Mayo's work also represents the first documented research involving women in the workplace. Perhaps its most important contribution was the assertion that those closest to the work often know more about it than leadership and that listening to them leads to better outcomes. Leaders who listen gain referent power and are better positioned to improve results.

Modern team practices and culture-building largely stem from Mayo's findings. He observed that people align their behavior with their peers and leaders; today, tools such as team charters, peer mentorship, and public praise leverage this group instinct explicitly.

But like Taylor, Mayo's approach had limitations. Pure democratic leadership isn't ideal in every situation. It works best when people are skilled and experienced and have time to discuss and innovate. It stalls when followers are inexperienced (what Marshall Goldsmith called "pooling ignorance") and can frustrate high performers who don't want prolonged debate. Most critically, democratic decision-making is slow. In urgent contexts, such as a Coast Guard rescue, deliberation can cost lives. Sometimes the most supportive thing a leader can do is tell someone exactly what to do.

But by and large, by the mid-twentieth century, two opposing approaches dominated leadership thinking: Taylor's autocratic system and Mayo's democratic one. Taylor emphasized tasks; Mayo emphasized people. You were either task-first or people-first, and studies kept multiplying, but the divide remained. Neither theory alone solved every leadership challenge.

We were beginning to see the real problem: One style doesn't fit all. Autocratic works sometimes. Democratic works sometimes. The challenge was knowing when. In the late 1940s, researchers commissioned by Ralph Stogdill at Ohio State University set out to resolve this dilemma once and for all.

Stogdill and the Two-Axis Breakthrough

Stogdill's early leadership research in the 1940s began with a simple question: *Are good leaders born or made?* A career academician and researcher, he was one of the first to challenge what was commonly known as trait-based leadership theory—the belief that leaders are born, not developed. His findings revealed that inborn traits alone couldn't explain leadership. A person might lead in one situation and follow in another, and leadership was, in fact, *learnable.*

That raised the next question: If leadership can be learned, what should leaders actually be trained to do? Should they apply Taylor's structured, directive methods, or adopt Mayo's more inclusive, relationship-driven approach?

With that in mind, Stogdill commissioned the Bureau of Business Research at Ohio State University to run one of the most ambitious leadership studies ever conducted. They analyzed tens of thousands of managers across several industries over a decade, evaluating their leadership along the following two criteria:

1. **Results**: Was the manager successful? Did the team or group hit their productivity targets and deliver targeted outcomes?
2. **Engagement**: Did people like working for this person? Did they feel supported and respected? Would they choose to work with this manager again?

These measures may look familiar because they mirror how we described the impact of leadership back in chapter 1—success, engagement, and retention. Stogdill's original research helped establish these as reliable ways to evaluate a leader's effectiveness.

Stogdill and his team expected to find a clear trait—several, perhaps—that led to leadership success. (They even hypothesized that Mayo's democratic style would be the reigning champion.) But after analyzing the data, it became clear that no single characteristic made someone an effective leader. Height, personality, communication style, temperament—none consistently predicted success. The same was true for leadership approach. Autocratic and democratic leaders could both get results; neither style consistently outperformed the other.

The data also surfaced a third approach, what the researchers called "laissez-faire," and what we would now describe as delegation or empowerment. Even then, it wasn't universally effective. Taken together, the Ohio State studies showed that there is no "one best leadership style"; the best leadership style *depends*.

The impact of this work was profound. Leaders didn't have to choose. Autocratic, democratic, and even laissez-faire leaders were all found to be both successful and effective in the right circumstances. That's when researchers began shifting away from personality-based theories and toward observable behaviors. The studies also produced the first well-known four-box leadership model, built on two independent dimensions.

- **Structure**: Echoing Taylor and scientific management. The extent to which a leader clarifies roles, goals, processes, and expectations. (This corresponds to what we now call task behavior—the x-axis of the Situational Leadership® Model.)
- **Consideration**: Echoing Mayo and human relations. The extent to which a leader asks questions, listens, and demonstrates support. (This corresponds to what we now call relationship behavior—the y-axis of the model.)

At the time researchers were surprised to discover that leaders could be high or low on either axis. In other words the two continuums weren't opposites but independent behaviors. A leader could demonstrate strong structure, strong consideration, both, or neither. That insight may feel obvious now, but it was a breakthrough at the time. It confirmed that there was no one best leadership style and created the behavioral backbone for what would eventually become the Situational Leadership® Model.

But there was still a deeper question researchers hadn't answered: *Why do leaders choose to behave the way they do?* If a leader could direct or involve others, empower, or guide, what determined the approach they reached for? That's where Douglas McGregor stepped in.

McGregor and the Mindset Behind Leadership Styles

Douglas McGregor, a research professor at MIT's Sloan School of Management in the 1950s and 1960s, expanded the field's focus beyond behaviors to examine the assumptions leaders hold about people. In *The Human Side of Enterprise*, he explored how a leader's underlying attitude shaped culture, expectations, and work itself. Building on the foundational work of Taylor and Mayo, McGregor articulated two contrasting mindsets about human motivation: Theory X and Theory Y.

From a Theory X standpoint, most people find work inherently unpleasant. They aren't ambitious or creative, prefer to avoid responsibility, and want to be directed and closely supervised. They seek security and the path of least resistance. Leaders operating from a Theory X mindset naturally adopt a strong, top-down approach: tight oversight, strict rules, clear consequences, and heavy control.

Theory Y, by contrast, assumed that, under the right conditions, all people were capable of self-direction and creativity. They want to learn, grow, and take responsibility. In organizations grounded in a Theory Y mindset, leaders guide development by providing structure when needed, offering feedback, creating opportunities for autonomy, and helping workers connect personal accomplishment with meaningful contribution. Motivation comes largely through positive reinforcement and trust.

These assumptions created two very different workplace cultures. A Theory X environment, with its command-and-control mindset, would produce one type of behavior among leaders and followers. A Theory Y environment—open, participative, developmental—would produce another.

McGregor concluded that Theory X organizations were becoming increasingly fragile in their modern era. In a society with rising levels of education and economic security, workers' basic needs were generally met; they had more potential and greater aspirations than Theory X assumed. And they no longer responded well to command-and-control management.

By contrast Theory Y offered a path that supported deeper human needs. In these environments people could become more self-motivated, creative, and autonomous, contributing to broader organizational goals.

Still, McGregor was careful to emphasize what Theory Y was not. It didn't claim that everyone is naturally self-motivated and creative; rather, it held that everyone *has the potential to be*. The leader's role, then, is to help unlock that potential.

McGregor also believed that the mindset of upper management shaped the culture and that Theory Y was the more accurate and effective way to view people (a belief research has largely supported over the years). Where his hypothesis fell short was in assuming that a particular mindset automatically produced a particular leadership style. In practice a Theory Y mindset didn't always lead to participative or empowering behavior, and a Theory X mindset didn't always result in strict control.

Likewise, Theory X and Theory Y were not a one-to-one match with directive or participative behavior. For example, a leader could hold a Theory Y mindset—believing in people's capability and potential—and still provide firm direction when needed. A project manager with a naturally directive style might correct, structure, or guide not because they think their workers are incapable but because that direction helps them succeed. This distinction became a key insight: *Attitudes and behaviors are not the same.* A leader's mindset doesn't predetermine their behavioral response.

McGregor's influence extended well beyond his era. Later thinkers—including Daniel Pink, with his focus on autonomy, mastery, and purpose—drew heavily from Theory Y. Contemporary approaches such as servant leadership, transformational leadership, flat hierarchies, team-based structures, and Agile methodologies all reflect Theory Y assumptions. Carol Dweck's research on fixed and growth mindsets also echoes McGregor's conclusions: People either believe that abilities are static or that they can be developed. A growth mindset, which views talents and abilities as improvable, predicts higher achievement, greater willingness to take risks, and higher levels of effort and learning.

McGregor's work also set an important foundation for the Situational Leadership® Model: Without a Theory Y mindset, the model doesn't work. Situational Leaders assume the best in people. They believe that individuals can learn, improve, and grow—and that their development is worth investing in. That mindset is constant, even as the leader flexes between all four leadership styles based on what the follower needs. In other words all four styles can be used with a Theory Y mindset because the leader's behavior shifts, but their belief in people's potential does not.

> *Situational Leaders assume the best in people. They believe that individuals can learn, improve, and grow—and that their development is worth investing in.*

Now we can start to see where the Situational Leadership® Model really begins to take shape. And it makes sense—because shortly after McGregor's research was published, Hersey was stepping onto the scene.

Matching Styles Brings Out the Best in People

Leaders who operate from Theory Y assumptions focus on growth, believing people can learn, develop, and contribute at high levels when given the right support. That's why each leadership style in the Situational Leadership® Model has a place: Every style aligns with what the follower needs for a specific task. Theory X assumptions, on the other hand, tend to shut down growth and, over time, push high performers out the door.

Consider two common situations. When a new worker is being onboarded, the leader should offer clear direction and close supervision. But when a seasoned performer starts doubting herself on a task she's already mastered, that same leader should shift into a more participative approach—talking through what's causing the insecurity and helping restore momentum. In both cases the leader's response is grounded in a belief that people can learn, grow, and contribute at high levels when supported in the right way.

The Top Half of the Model

In the 1960s Hersey was just beginning to put the puzzle pieces together that would eventually become the Situational Leadership® Model. If you take a quick peek at the top half, you'll begin to see how he integrated decades of research into identifying four distinct leadership styles.

- From Taylor, it carried forward the importance of task behavior: providing clarity, structure, and direction.
- From Mayo, it drew on the significance of relationship behavior: listening, supporting, and involving others.
- From Stogdill and the Ohio State studies, it reinforced that these behaviors were independent dimensions, not opposites.
- And from McGregor, it recognized that leaders' assumptions about people didn't necessarily align with a particular leadership style.

Taken together, these insights formed the backbone of the model's top half. The four styles—S1, S2, S3, and S4—naturally emerged from the different combinations of task and relationship behavior, just as the Ohio State researchers first mapped in their original four-box grid. Each style represents a distinct blend of the two behaviors.

Instead of prescribing one "best" way to lead, the model reflected what the research had been saying all along: Effective leadership depends on matching the right style to the situation.

But that's only half the story. Everything you've just read accounts for how the leadership-style side of the model came to be. To complete the picture, we still need to understand the other half—the historical foundations of Performance Readiness® and why it became the driving force of the Situational Leadership® Model. That's the next chapter in our historical adventure.

Chapter 3 Review

Here are the key takeaways from chapter 3:

- This chapter introduces the research that shaped the leadership-style portion of the Situational Leadership® Model.
- Frederick Taylor's scientific management established the foundation for task behavior—clarity, direction, structure, and efficiency.
- Elton Mayo's human relations research introduced the importance of relationship behavior—listening, involvement, and support.
- Ralph Stogdill and the Ohio State studies confirmed that task and relationship behaviors are independent dimensions and that no single leadership style works in every situation.
- Douglas McGregor showed how a leader's assumptions about people (Theory X versus Theory Y) shape culture. A Theory Y mindset is essential for Situational Leadership® because it assumes people can learn, grow, and develop.
- Together, these insights form the backbone of the model's four leadership styles, explaining how and why leaders vary their approach.
- The defining contribution was integrating these findings into a practical, behavioral framework—what became the top half of the Situational Leadership® Model.

The Roots of Readiness

For the first fifty years of leadership research, leadership and human motivation were studied separately, as if they belonged to completely different domains. Odd in retrospect, but that's how the field evolved. Situational Leadership® was one of the first contingency-based models to bring those two worlds together.

Which brings us to the other half of the model: the follower.

If leaders are expected to flex their behavior, what causes followers to need more direction in one moment and more support in another? Why do some situations require clarity, while others demand encouragement? Why do follower needs shift—sometimes gradually, sometimes suddenly?

Situations differ because tasks differ and because followers change. People's needs aren't fixed; they evolve as an individual gains experience, builds confidence, or encounters new challenges. To understand how and why those needs shift, we turn to the origins of Performance Readiness®.

That path begins with Chris Argyris.

Argyris and How People Develop

Chris Argyris, a professor at Yale and later Harvard Business School, devoted his career to understanding how people learn and grow within organizations. His work helped clarify the important distinction Mc-Gregor identified: Mindset isn't the same as behavior.

McGregor had introduced Theory X and Theory Y as opposing sets of assumptions that leaders hold about people. In the mid-1960s, Argyris extended that thinking by identifying two corresponding behavior sets: A and B. Type A behaviors, commonly associated with Theory X, reflected low openness: Leaders didn't own their feelings, resisted trying new approaches, and relied on control and distrust. Type B behaviors, aligned with Theory Y, reflected greater openness and support: Leaders experimented, acknowledged emotions, helped others, and built trust.

However, Argyris stressed that mindset and behavior didn't always align. A Theory X leader might behave supportively for selfish reasons, and a Theory Y leader might provide firm structure for a short period if people lacked skill or confidence. This reinforced the critical insight that assumptions and behaviors are related, but one doesn't predict or dictate the other.

Argyris later shifted his research focus from leaders to followers. Drawing on childhood development research, he proposed that individuals mature over time, both personally and professionally, through a progression he called the immaturity-maturity continuum. He described seven developmental shifts.

- Passive → Active
- Dependent → Independent
- Behave in a few ways → Behave in many ways
- Shallow interests → Deep interests
- Short-term perspective → Past-and-future perspective
- Subordinate position → Equal or superior position
- Low self-awareness → High self-awareness and self-control

Maturity, Argyris observed, develops gradually and unevenly. People may be more "mature" in some areas than others, and culture can either accelerate or limit that growth. When workers appeared apathetic or unmotivated, the problem often wasn't the people themselves; it was the environment—systems that kept them passive or dependent, or boredom that set in once they'd mastered a task and no longer felt challenged.

The same principle applies to development at work. Just as parents provide structure for infants and gradually reduce direction as children grow, leaders should adjust their support as followers gain ability and confidence. Treating someone as "immature" when they've already developed is about as useful as changing a teenager's diapers (what we would eventually call a mismatch).

The Situational Leadership® Model draws heavily from this continuum. Argyris's insights helped shape what we now call Performance Readiness®.

- Followers who are still learning a task (R1, R2) demonstrate immaturity.
- Followers who have built competence (R3, R4) demonstrate maturity.

If supported, people naturally grow. With feedback, encouragement, and opportunities to learn, they gain new skills and develop confidence. Leaders accelerate that process by adjusting style over time, helping people mature within the task and context.

Time to Autonomy

Argyris showed that people naturally develop from dependence to independence when supported. In organizations this journey is measured through "time to autonomy"—how long it takes a new contributor to build the ability and confidence to perform complex tasks with little guidance.

We'll explore this idea in more depth in chapter 10, but for now it's enough to understand that when leaders actively support that development, followers gain mastery faster. Mastering Performance Readiness® gives organizations a real competitive edge. At CLS, we call this "turning potential into performance."

Argyris helped us understand how people grow in Performance Readiness® over time. But as a reminder, Performance Readiness® isn't only about what people can do. It's also about what they're *willing* to do—their confidence, commitment, and motivation for the specific task. Hersey used to refer to ability and willingness as "an interactive influence system." The more ability you had, the more confident and motivated you tended to be when it came time to demonstrate it. The more willingness you had, the quicker you'd develop ability.

To understand more about why willingness varies from person to person (and task to task), we turn to another influential thinker who focused on human development, Abraham Maslow.

Maslow and the Essence of Willingness

Our behavior—at work, at school, and everywhere in between—is shaped by our deepest-felt needs at that moment. We act because we want something, or because we value something, or even because we're trying to avoid something. A nurse may take an extra shift to meet a need for financial security, while another volunteers for overtime because they want to help out in a time of need. A team member may speak up in a meeting to fulfill a need for contribution or recognition, while another stays quiet to avoid feeling exposed or vulnerable.

Abraham Maslow, one of the most influential voices in behavioral science, spent his career studying those needs. In 1943 he published what became known as the "hierarchy of needs," a framework suggesting that some human needs carry more weight than others and that we satisfy the most essential ones before pursuing higher-order ones.

self-
actualization
realizing personal
potential, self-fulfillment,
seeking personal growth
and peak experiences

self-esteem
self-esteem, achievement, mastery,
independence, status, dominance,
prestige, responsibility

love and belonging
friendship, intimacy, affection, and love

safety and security
protection from elements, security, order, law, stability

physiological needs
air, food, drink, shelter, warmth, sex, sleep

Maslow described five core human needs.

1. **Physiological:** Basic survival needs such as food, water, shelter, and rest. When these aren't met, it's hard to focus on anything else.
2. **Safety:** Stability and protection. This includes having a plan or system in place for emergencies.
3. **Social/belonging:** Connection and community. People want relationships that bring enjoyment, support, and a sense of inclusion.
4. **Self-esteem:** Feeling capable and valued. People want to take pride in their work and be ecognized for their contributions.
5. **Self-actualization:** Purpose, growth, and realizing potential. This is the sense that you're doing what you're meant to do.

Maslow arranged these needs in a pyramid based on what he called "prepotency." In other words until the more basic needs—physiological and safety—are at least adequately met, it's difficult for someone to focus on the higher-level ones. (There are exceptions, of course, such as individuals who sacrifice basic needs for a cause they deeply believe in.)

Importantly, people don't have to be perfectly satisfied at one level to care about the next, just satisfied enough. In any given moment, we pursue the need that feels most pressing. And that highest-felt need explains not just what someone is doing but *why* they're doing it.

At work this is key because many people in modern society have already satisfied their physiological and safety needs. As McGregor observed, they're often looking to their work to meet needs for belonging, recognition, achievement, purpose, and personal growth. This challenges the old assumption that people are naturally lazy, complacent, or uninterested in leadership. In reality most people want to stretch themselves, be creative, take on responsibility, and pursue a greater purpose.

Work becomes more motivating when it helps people satisfy these higher-order needs. That insight helps explain Theory Y: Under the right conditions, people will learn, grow, and contribute because work, like play, becomes a meaningful outlet for reaching their potential.

Maslow's ideas influenced countless fields: psychology, health care, education, business, you name it. Amy Edmondson pulls from Maslow's hierarchy in *The Fearless Organization*, where she talks about psychological safety at work. When people feel safe to speak up, they collaborate, innovate, and contribute more, a direct reflection of social and self-esteem needs.

Daniel Pink's *Drive* builds on that same foundation, describing three elements that unlock motivation: autonomy (the ability to direct your own work), mastery (the desire to become skilled), and purpose (the sense that your work contributes to something meaningful). These drivers align closely with Maslow's higher-order needs at the top of the pyramid. Organizations that support them tend to attract and retain people who take pride in their work and consistently contribute at a high level.

Understanding a follower's highest-felt need helps leaders connect the work to what motivates that person most. A software engineer who turns down a higher-paying job to stay on a small innovation team isn't choosing money; she's choosing creativity and impact. Others may be fueled by autonomy, recognition, mastery, purpose, or belonging. Different people value different things, which means their motivation, and therefore their *willingness*, will vary.

In fact, insecurity or unwillingness often reflects an unmet need. When someone hesitates, resists, or pulls back, the issue is rarely laziness. More often, something essential isn't being satisfied. That's why, in the four steps of the model, we emphasize diagnosing the source of unwillingness by identifying the follower's strongest-felt need, whether that's confidence, commitment, or motivation. Maslow's hierarchy offers a helpful lens.

Insecurity may signal unmet needs for the following:

- **Safety and security:** Fear of failing publicly or losing credibility
- **Belonging:** Worry about disappointing the team
- **Self-esteem:** Doubts about ability or readiness

Unwillingness often stems from unmet needs for the following:

- **Safety:** Believing the task is risky or sets them up to fail
- **Self-actualization:** Feeling the task doesn't align with their goals, values, or sense of meaningful work

Different unmet needs lead to different reactions. When leaders understand what's beneath the behavior, they can respond in ways that restore willingness and help the performer move forward.

Maslow helped us understand the broad landscape of human needs and how they shape motivation. But those insights raised another question for the workplace: What makes someone feel motivated at work, and what shuts that motivation down? That's where, in the 1960s, Frederick Herzberg picked up the thread.

Herzberg and Motivation

In the Pittsburgh area in the mid-1950s, Herzberg rallied a team to study needs and motivation in the workplace. They interviewed two hundred engineers and accountants, asking what satisfied and dissatisfied them about their work, and the results were surprising. Herzberg assumed there would be one list—a single set of factors that, when present, motivated people and, when absent, led to dissatisfaction. If you had "it," you were motivated; if you didn't, you weren't.

Instead, he uncovered two distinct categories: what "turned people on" at work and what "turned them off." The factors that motivated people weren't the same factors that demotivated them!

He discovered that people felt most satisfied when they were doing work with meaning and challenge. They were energized by opportunities for responsibility, growth, and making meaningful contributions. These became known as "motivators."

Equally important were the factors that produced dissatisfaction: the lack of fair pay, adequate tools, and constructive relationships. Herzberg compared these to hygiene: When present, they weren't particularly noticeable, but when absent, they ruined the work experience. In other words fair pay and great tools didn't create satisfaction on their own, but without them, workers struggled to feel motivated.

Herzberg's findings aligned closely with Maslow's. Lower-order needs—survival, safety, and social belonging—must be met, or they drown out everything else. But once those needs are "good enough," employees look for higher-order needs: growth, recognition, and purpose. In other words meeting hygiene factors simply clears the way for those deeper motivators to rise.

Modern organizations continue to reflect Herzberg's insights. Competitive pay, benefits, healthy workplace relationships, the right tools, and flexible environments may seem ordinary, but without them, satisfaction and performance quickly erode. Yet hygiene alone isn't enough. The most successful organizations also create opportunities for autonomy, mastery, purpose, and, in Herzberg's terms, "the chance to make meaningful contributions."

Herzberg's influence shows up in later work, including Marcus Buckingham's *First, Break All the Rules* and Gallup's ongoing Q12 research. Those studies translate motivators and hygiene factors into measurable, manager-focused questions, such as "Do I have the opportunity to do what I do best every day?" and "Does someone at work care about me?" Gallup continues to replicate Herzberg's findings year after year. Although the workplace has changed, purpose, meaningful work, and autonomy are still core drivers of workplace motivation.

For leaders, the takeaway is simple: The more you understand what drives each person, the more effectively you can support the willingness side of Performance Readiness®. When you understand what's important to someone, you can better anticipate their behavior. You can ask better questions. And you can create an environment that fosters motivation and engagement. This helps leaders attract, hire, develop, and retain people by supporting their drive to grow, contribute, and perform at their best.

> *The more you understand what drives each person, the more effectively you can support the willingness side of Performance Readiness®.*

The Model Is Born

As research on leadership and human development evolved along separate paths, a young college professor in the 1960s found himself teaching a course on leadership studies at Ohio University.

As he prepared his syllabus, he organized the most influential research of the time into two distinct sections. The first reviewed the most meaningful contributions from researchers who studied leaders. The second reviewed the most meaningful contributions from researchers who studied human development and motivation. The final exam was a blue-book essay asking students to identify and explain the central themes and practical essence of each theory from both sections.

A Lasting Friendship

In the mid-1960s, Hersey was teaching organizational behavior at Ohio University. His course quickly became one of the most talked-about classes on campus, so much so that you had to register early just to get in. A newly hired professor, Dr. Ken Blanchard, kept hearing about it and wanted to see what the buzz was about. He introduced himself and asked if he could audit the course.

Hersey famously replied, "No one audits my class . . . but I'll figure out a way to make sure you can get enrolled." That semester sparked a partnership and lifelong friendship.

The classroom became a kind of laboratory for what would eventually become a new way of thinking about leadership. Hersey and Blanchard began developing a framework called Life Cycles of Leadership, first published in the *Training and Development Journal* in May 1969. Over the next several years, they continued testing and refining the concept through the first three editions of their textbook, *Management of Organizational Behavior*. By the fourth edition, published in 1982 by Prentice Hall, the framework was renamed the Situational Leadership® Model.

Here's a replica of the guide that professor used to grade those exams:

Leadership Research

- **Frederick Winslow Taylor:** Scientific management—The role of the leader is to make decisions and tell workers what to do and how to do it.
- **Elton Mayo:** Human relations theory—The role of the leader is to recognize the power of the team in determining what to do and how to do it.

- **Ralph Stogdill:** Ohio State studies—There are no traits that predict who leaders will be and no best style of leadership.
- **Douglas McGregor:** Theory X and Theory Y—The assumptions that leaders have about followers are significant, and successful leaders adopt Theory Y assumptions.

Human Development and Motivation Research

- **Chris Argyris:** Maturity-immaturity theory—The more familiar followers become with a task, the more their confidence and perspective grow/mature.
- **Abraham Maslow:** Hierarchy of needs—People have different needs arranged in a hierarchy, and the strongest-felt need at any moment drives behavior.
- **Frederick Herzberg:** Motivation–hygiene theory—The things that "turn people on" at work are different from the things that "turn them off."

Then came a magical moment.

It began with placing Argyris's maturity-immaturity continuum directly beneath the four-box model from the Ohio State studies. The professor and one of his students took a closer look at the course curriculum. "What if we combined Section 1 with Section 2?"

Suddenly, that young professor began to see something nobody else had pulled together: These weren't two unrelated bodies of knowledge. They were two halves of the same story.

What leaders did and what followers needed were inseparable.

Something clicked.

Those two halves—leadership behavior and follower development— fit together in a way the field had never articulated. And from that moment, the Situational Leadership® Model began to take shape.

The rest, as they say, is history.

But now it's time to bring that history into the present. Because while we can trace the research behind the Situational Leadership® Model back to the early thinkers you've just met, the real transformation happens when you begin to put the pieces together. Over the next few chapters, we'll do just that: walk through all four steps of the Situational Leadership® Model. As we do, you'll start to see the model the same way Hersey did all those years ago, as a practical, repeatable, tool leaders can use to effectively influence others.

> ❝ *What leaders did and what followers needed were inseparable.*

In the next chapter, we'll take the first step by learning how to clearly identify the specific task.

Chapter 4 Review

Here are the key takeaways from chapter 4:

- This chapter introduces the research that shaped the follower portion of the Situational Leadership® Model: Performance Readiness®.
- Early theorists studied leadership and human development separately; the breakthrough came when those two bodies of research were combined.
- Chris Argyris's work showed that people develop ability and confidence over time and that leaders must adjust direction and support as followers grow.
- Abraham Maslow's hierarchy highlighted how motivation, and therefore willingness, shifts based on a person's strongest-felt need.
- Frederick Herzberg demonstrated that the factors that motivate people differ from the factors that prevent dissatisfaction, deepening our understanding of willingness at work.
- Together, these ideas form the foundation of Performance Readiness® by explaining why ability and willingness change across tasks and situations.

- Recognizing that leadership behavior and follower development are inseparable was an insight that evolved into the Situational Leadership® Model.

Reflect and Apply

Before you move on, take a moment to reflect on how this chapter applies to your leadership today.

1. Which idea—Argyris, Maslow, or Herzberg—best helps you understand why someone on your team needs more direction or more support right now?
2. Think of a follower whose willingness has shifted recently. What need might be influencing their motivation, and how could you address it?

Same-Page Status

Step One: Identify the Specific Task

Imagine you go to the doctor because you haven't been feeling well. He asks a few questions, listens carefully, and runs some tests. A few days later, he reviews the results and prescribes medication. But instead of getting better, you start to feel worse, and new symptoms show up. Now you're not only still sick but actually *sicker* and understandably really frustrated.

Does that mean the medication was bad? Probably not. More likely, the diagnosis was off. The doctor treated the wrong problem. Even though he followed the process, asked good questions, and felt confident in the treatment plan, nothing improved because the root cause was never accurately identified.

Leadership works much the same way.

When we misdiagnose a situation, there's a slim chance we'll influence effectively. And one of the easiest places to misdiagnose is right at the beginning, around the task itself. If you have one picture of completion in your head and the performer has another, you're not aligned on a picture of success. If you're leading the performer at the level of big goals when the performer needs details on the task, you're both aiming at different targets.

That's why diagnosis is the first skill to master in the Situational Leadership® Model. And it begins with getting crystal clear on the task, setting the stage for the next few steps that we'll cover in the following chapters.

The Situational Leadership® Model has four steps.

1. Identify the specific task.
2. Assess current Performance Readiness®.
3. Match and communicate leader response.
4. Manage the movement.

The first two steps make up the diagnostic work. A full diagnosis of a situation involves both defining the task with enough specificity that everyone knows what "good" looks like and then evaluating the performer's ability and willingness to execute that clearly defined task. You can't do the second without doing the first.

In this chapter we'll focus on Step One: Identify the Specific Task. This is where alignment begins. When the leader and performer share the same understanding of the work and the standard for success, everything that follows becomes easier and more effective.

> *Situational Leadership®*
> *is the language of alignment.*

Clarity Begins with the Task

Situational Leadership® is the language of alignment, and alignment starts with getting clear on the work itself. Back in chapter 2, we introduced the idea that this model is always task-specific. Someone isn't simply "ready" or "not ready" in general; they're ready for this particular task. Because the model is task-specific, it gives both the leader and the performer an objective starting point they can rally around. If we don't know what we're aiming at, nothing that follows will land the way we hope.

Defining the task sounds obvious, but believe us—it's far from easy. Some tasks are straightforward: Paint this wall, enter this data, close this account. Others are more abstract: Take initiative, lead this project, improve communication with the client. The more abstract the task, the more intentional we must be in defining what "success" looks like. This step is about making sure we're all talking about the same thing so everyone understands what "done well" actually means.

Think about how it feels to pour time and energy into something, only to learn later that you missed the mark because expectations weren't clear. It's discouraging and frustrating. Remember Herzberg's research on motivators and demotivators? Alignment on the task functions much like a "hygiene factor," easy to overlook when it's present but painfully obvious when it's not. Leaders sometimes skip Step One because they assume the follower sees the same picture they do. But when alignment is missing, missteps follow, undermining both success and engagement.

When a leader and a performer achieve what we call *same-page status*—shared clarity about the task and what "done well" looks like—they're united around one vision with a clear road map for execution. Without same-page status, we start to see confusion creeping in, performance stalling, and confidence eroding.

Same-page status
When the leader and follower share clarity
about the specific task and what an acceptable
level of performance looks like

Creating same-page status requires communication. One of the fastest ways to check alignment is to ask the performer to describe the task in their own words. If their understanding matches yours, great. If not, you've uncovered the gap early and can course correct before real work begins. Weekly one-on-ones, daily stand-ups, short check-ins, anything that creates space to confirm expectations, track progress, and identify obstacles.

A helpful mindset shift is this: We don't lead a person; we lead a person *for a task*. With practice this becomes second nature. Over time leaders learn how much clarity a performer needs and when.

The Situational Leadership® Model is built on four essential skills every leader must master: **diagnose, adapt, communicate, and advance**.

The first, and arguably most critical, is diagnosing: the ability to read the situation before reacting to it. Diagnosing means understanding what's really happening, both the specific task and the person doing it. When you accurately assess competence and commitment, you can respond with intention instead of assumption.

You'll use the skill of diagnosing to define the specific task in Step One and to assess Performance Readiness® in Step Two. It's the skill that sets up everything else in the model.

Putting Step One into Practice

To see how Step One works in real life, let's look at Hana—a director of product innovation—and Michael, a senior developer on her team. You'll follow them across the next few chapters as they move through the Situational Leadership® process together.

Hana has been with the organization for eight years and has spent the past three overseeing product innovation. She began as a junior developer and moved into leadership because she delivers results, develops and retains talent, works well across functions, and builds trust with her people. Her natural leadership style leans S3, participating. She's always inviting input, synthesizing concerns, and helping others take thoughtful next steps.

Michael is highly creative with deep experience in app development. He has a strong track record and is well respected across the organization. He prides himself on "going away" to build and then reappearing with excellent finished work. At a high level, Michael's latest assignment is to develop an app that allows clients to access key content on the go.

As Hana prepares for Step One (identifying the specific task), she clarifies what successful performance will require. On the surface this project looks simple. But as she thinks it through, she realizes it's bigger than writing clean code. Michael will be working within a cross-functional group, receiving feedback in the moment, refining ideas, and ensuring the final experience meets client needs.

At this stage Hana identifies one primary task: Build the app in partnership with stakeholders across the organization. Michael is thrilled. This is exactly the kind of creative challenge he's been waiting for! Heading into the first stakeholder meeting, he prepares a talk track he's sure will "wow" the group.

At first things go well, and he presents confidently. But as the group begins providing feedback to build on his proposal—sharing ideas and asking clarifying questions—Michael starts to shut down. He grows defensive and withdraws, distancing himself from the discussion. His engagement fades; if the group just wants him to take orders, *fine*.

For Hana, this moment signals something important: There's more than one task at play. Yes, Michael is responsible for building the app. But he also has to collaborate in real time, respond to input, and adjust ideas alongside others. That additional layer—receiving feedback in the moment on development ideas—is now central to the success of the work. Hana notes this as part of Step One because these expectations directly affect how she'll assess Michael's Performance Readiness®.

Forest → Tree → Leaf

A simple way to identify the right task is the forest → tree → leaf analogy. It gives us a way to zoom in or out, until we find the level that creates shared clarity.

At the forest level, we're talking about someone's role. Titles such as operations manager or senior analyst help set the stage, but a role is far too broad to guide day-to-day influence. We call this the "overall level" because we're looking at a person's role as a whole rather than breaking it down. And generally speaking, we can't lead someone well based solely on the job they hold.

At the tree level, we're looking at a person's objectives or key performance goals. We call this the "major level" because it focuses on major priorities and milestones such as launching a new product, improving customer experience, stabilizing revenue, and so on. It provides helpful context, but it still may not be specific enough for real-time leadership decisions.

Sometimes we need to zoom all the way to the leaf level—the specific tasks required to accomplish the objective. You can also think of this as the "detailed level," where we get into the minutiae of the work. This is where we really sharpen clarity: Build the launch schedule, run weekly customer calls, create the pricing model. We won't always need leaf-level detail, but depending on the situation or the person, we might. The goal is to define the task clearly enough that both the leader and the performer understand what a "sustained, acceptable level" of performance looks like as defined by the leader (the person responsible for measuring success and outcomes).

Forest → Tree → Leaf Example

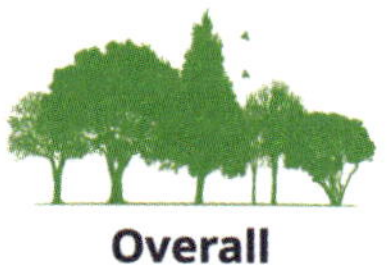

Overall
Job or Role

Detailed
Activity or Task

Major
Performance Goal
or Objective

Here's an example of how to break down a task to the forest, tree, and leaf level:

1. **Describe the job or role.**

    Middle School English Teacher

2. **List three performance goals or objectives that are a part of the job.**

    - Deliver grade-level English curriculum aligned with state standards.
    - Assess and track student progress.
    - Maintain a classroom environment that supports learning and engagement.

3. **Choose one objective and list three to five activities or tasks related to that objective.** Describe each task in detail, including expectations for successful performance.

    Objective: Deliver grade-level English curriculum aligned with state standards.

    - Create daily lesson plans that include clear learning objectives, engaging activities, differentiated support for diverse learners, and an assessment strategy.
    - Facilitate class discussions and instructional activities that help students build reading comprehension, writing skills, and critical thinking.
    - Design and deliver writing assignments that teach students how to analyze texts, organize ideas, and revise their work.
    - Integrate state test preparation into the curriculum by using sample passages, modeling strategies, and providing guided practice.

That's exactly what Hana did with Michael. The forest was his role as senior developer. The tree was the broader initiative: Build an app that delivers key content on the go. But staying at the tree would have left too much room for assumptions. To ensure alignment, she zoomed to the leaf level and clarified two specific tasks required to move the work forward.

- Build the app in partnership with stakeholders.
- Receive feedback in the moment.

Only at the leaf level would both Hana and Michael gain shared clarity about what success required both technically and relationally.

Step Two depends on this level of shared clarity. You can't accurately diagnose someone's Performance Readiness® if you're unclear about the task itself. When the task is fuzzy, your assessment will be too. But when the task is defined at the right level that's specific enough to set expectations, readiness becomes far easier to evaluate objectively.

By identifying the task at the leaf level, Hana ensured she and Michael were on the same page before moving forward. And now, with shared clarity in place, she and Michael are ready to align on his Performance Readiness® for each part of the work.

Two Common Mistakes

Leaders often trip over Step One in a few predictable ways. Here are the two most common:

1. Assuming clarity: Leaders describe a task at a high level because they understand it so well, and they unintentionally leave others to fill in the blanks. This leads to misalignment and rework.

2. Overexplaining: Sometimes leaders provide far more detail about the task when the performer already understands the details. Time is wasted breaking the task down to this level.

The goal is to find the right level of specificity for the person and the situation—enough clarity to create alignment without overwhelming or underinforming. Here are some tips to avoid these mistakes:

- Consider the performer's experience: Have they completed this task many times? If so, you likely don't need to get to the detailed leaf level for them. They already know what good looks like.
- Check for understanding along the way. You might start at the overall level for a task and then pause to check for understanding. If you're on the same page, you can stop here. If not, keep digging deeper.

Figuring It Out Together

The examples we've shared so far represent some of the day-to-day tasks leaders and performers face. But we all know the "day-to-day" goes out the window when change comes along or a new opportunity emerges that requires your team's engagement.

If you're on the cutting edge of your industry or trying to stay up to date with the newest technology, you've likely worked with tasks you don't fully understand. That can trigger stress, anxiety, and even impostor syndrome for both leaders and followers. And it makes Step One far more complicated. After all, how do you define a task in detail when you don't yet know what the details are?

In these situations identifying the specific task becomes an ongoing process rather than a onetime definition. To get started, you and the follower simply need to get to same-page status on *the next best step*, not on the entire process. Then regroup. Did that step produce the outcome you hoped for? What would you do differently? What did you learn? And from there, what's the next best step? As you and the performer continue to check in, you gradually build a shared under-standing of what good looks like for a task that's new to both of you.

This is a great reminder that the four steps in the Situational Leadership® Model aren't there for you to rush through and simply "check off." Each step is an opportunity for dialogue, a chance for you to be transparent as a leader about what you do or don't know. Step One, es-pecially, is an opportunity for you to share your point of view and then listen to the follower's perspective. When done well, identifying the task becomes a collaborative process where you and the follower craft a vision of success together and figure out the steps toward bringing that vision to life. That collaboration ultimately strengthens trust and alignment.

Now that you've defined the task—whether it's familiar, brand new, or still taking shape—you've established the foundation for ev-erything that comes next. Every decision in the Situational Leadership® Model flows from that shared understanding. Readiness isn't assessed in a vacuum; it's assessed in relation to *this* task, as you've defined it together. Once you're aligned on what "good" looks like, you can turn your attention to the performer and ask the crucial next question: Where are they today in their ability and willingness to carry out this specific task? That's the work of our next step.

Chapter 5 Review

Here are the key takeaways from chapter 5:

- Step One (Identify the Task) is the foundation of the Situational Leadership® Model.
- Situational Leadership® is task-specific. People aren't "ready" or "not ready" in general—they're ready for this task, at this moment.
- Leaders and performers must reach same-page status, a shared understanding of what the task is and what "done well" looks like.
- The forest → tree → leaf framework helps leaders find the right level of specificity, adjusting depth based on the person and situation.
- When tasks are new, ambiguous, or evolving, Step One becomes an ongoing process. Leaders and performers align on the next best step, check progress, and refine from there.
- Clear task definition, at the right level, creates the foundation for accurately assessing Performance Readiness® in Step Two.

Reflect and Apply

1. Choose a current task. Break it down at the forest, tree, and leaf levels. Which level provides the clarity your performer needs right now?
2. When a task is uncertain, how can you create same-page status on the next best step rather than the entire plan?
3. What conversations do you need to revisit to ensure you and your performers are aligned before moving forward?

Reading Behavior Cues

Step Two: Assess Current Performance Readiness®

Consider what it must be like to be a coach on *The Voice*. You're sitting in a chair turned away from the stage. You can't see the performer. You don't know their background, their training, or their relevant experience. You don't even know what they look like. All you have to go on is what they demonstrate in that moment—their voice (hence the title of the show!).

Your job is to diagnose what you hear and decide whether they've shown enough talent to move on to the next stage.

In the world of Situational Leadership®, leaders do pretty much the same thing, just without the spinning chairs and live audience. Once the task is clear, the leader's job is to diagnose the performer's readiness for that specific task. Thankfully, leaders have more cues than a single performance to work with. But the core responsibility is the same: Determine where the performer is right now and what they need to succeed.

We call this Performance Readiness®, a concept we first introduced in chapter 2 and are now putting into practice here.

And just like the coaches on *The Voice*, leaders can't rely on assumptions. They have to observe, listen, and diagnose the clues right in front of them. Misread readiness, and even the best leadership approach will fall flat. Diagnose it accurately, and you'll know exactly how to support the performer moving forward. So get your buzzers ready. In this chapter we'll explore what readiness looks like, how to assess it, and how a clear diagnosis sets you up to adapt your leadership style to what your follower needs.

Readiness Lives in the Task

Situational Leadership® is a follower-driven model, and this is where that becomes real. Rather than choosing a leadership style based on your preference or gut instinct, you're choosing based on what the performer needs to be successful with the specific task. The goal is alignment, understanding where the performer is today so you can meet them there.

You might remember that readiness has two components: ability and willingness. Now the focus shifts from understanding those concepts to diagnosing them in real time. That means tuning in, asking good questions, and paying attention to what the performer is actually demonstrating today (not what they did months ago and not what you hope they'll eventually be able to do).

Think about two different performers. One is enthusiastic about a new task but has limited experience. Another has done the task expertly for years. The assignment might sound identical (it might even look identical on paper!), but what each person needs from you at that moment is entirely different.

This kind of diagnosis often happens subtly. Performers don't usually announce, "I'm unsure" or "I'm overconfident." In fact, people often don't give you the full truth, even when you press. They may overstate their ability because they want to look competent, or they may say as little as possible because they don't want to look unprepared. That's why a thoughtful assessment isn't based only on what someone tells you. It's based on what you observe in their behavior.

If you think back to the physician example from the last chapter, diagnosing readiness works much the same way as a medical diagnosis. A good doctor doesn't just look at the numbers on a chart to make a diagnosis; they're listening to their patient, asking questions, picking up on nonverbal cues, connecting dots, and building a clearer picture of what's really happening. Good leaders do the same. They look for hesitation, pay attention to behavior, note whether action matches enthusiasm, and start stitching together a realistic read on what a performer needs next. That's diagnosis. And to do this well, you must ask the following two key questions:

1. Is the person currently performing?

This is an assessment of ability—the demonstrated knowledge, experience, or skill required to perform the task at a sustained, acceptable level today. Remember, ability isn't potential; it's what someone is consistently doing *right now*. If someone once mastered the task but hasn't touched it in a year, they may not be "able" in Situational Leadership® terms until they reacclimate.

2. Are they confident, committed, and/or motivated?

This is an assessment of willingness—the confidence, commitment, and motivation someone brings to the task. A performer may have strong skill yet hesitate because they lack confidence, feel overwhelmed at the moment, or have simply lost interest. Another may be eager and committed but still totally unsure of how to begin.

Together, these questions reveal where someone sits on that Performance Readiness® continuum we discussed.

- **R1: Unable and Insecure or Unwilling**
- **R2: Unable but Confident or Willing**
- **R3: Able but Insecure or Unwilling**
- **R4: Able and Confident and Willing**

Performance Readiness®

HIGH	MODERATE		LOW
R4	**R3**	**R2**	**R1**
Able and Confident and Willing ←	→ Able but Insecure or Unwilling	Unable but Confident or Willing ←	→ Unable and Insecure or Unwilling

Self Directed	Leader Directed

And here's the link back to Step One: The clearer the task, the easier it is to diagnose readiness accurately. When ability or willingness is unclear, it's often a sign that the task needs to be broken down further. Accurate diagnosis puts everything else in motion. It's the bridge between knowing the model and applying it to understand real people's needs.

Putting Step Two into Practice

Back to Hana and Michael. With the tasks defined, Hana now evaluates Michael's readiness to perform them today. Because the initiative has several moving parts, she considers the two tasks separately: (1) building the app, and (2) receiving real-time feedback on development ideas.

For building the app, Michael is energized and confident. In their last one-on-one, he told Hana he'd been sharing details about the project with his wife and even his neighbor. He sees this as a chance to prove himself and gain visibility. But this project is broader in scope than anything he's built before and requires cross-functional collaboration, something he hasn't done at this level.

So while he's enthusiastic and willing, he hasn't yet demonstrated the ability to perform this kind of work at a sustained, acceptable level. Hana assesses him as R2: Unable but Confident or Willing for this task.

The second task is different. It requires Michael to process input in real time, to engage collaboratively with other stakeholders. Historically, this hasn't been his rhythm. He prefers to work alone, keep his head down, and reappear with polished results.

During the most recent meeting, when teammates began asking

clarifying questions, Michael shut down. He pushed his chair back, stopped taking notes, got defensive, and even questioned whether the team was "ready for a project like this." His reaction signaled insecurity and resistance, the opposite of collaboration. For this part of the work, Hana assesses him as R1: Unable and Insecure or Unwilling.

She also knows it's very likely that Michael sees himself differently. She anticipates that their perspectives won't fully align and that this conversation will require both specificity and care. But she knows it needs to happen. She's concerned about the team's dynamic. She's committed to Michael's growth. And she knows that diagnosing where he truly is, task by task, is the only way to support him well moving forward.

What Hana Observes

Task: Build the App

As Hana considers Michael's readiness for the development work, she looks at what's *observable*, not assumptions or past reputation.

Facts (what's true about the task):

- This is a new app project.
- The scope is larger than anything he's built before.
- It requires cross-functional collaboration.

Behaviors (what she sees/hears):

- He's incredibly enthusiastic. (He's been telling his wife and even his neighbor about the project.)
- He's eager and sees this as a chance to showcase his abilities.
- He's highly engaged and confident he'll succeed.

Based on these observations, Hana anticipates Michael may self-assess as R4. But because he hasn't yet demonstrated his ability at this expanded scope, she places him at R2: Unable but Confident or Willing.

Task: Receive Feedback in the Moment

When Hana zooms in on how Michael handled real-time collaboration, she again focuses on what's observable.

Facts (what's true about the context):

- Michael typically works independently.
- The cross-functional team includes leads from every major department.
- It was clear the team didn't know how to interpret or respond to Michael's behavior during the meeting.

Behaviors (what she sees/hears):

- He pushed his chair back and physically disengaged from the group.
- He stopped taking notes.
- He became defensive when asked clarifying questions.
- He questioned whether the team was "even ready for a project like this."

These observations point to R1: Unable and Insecure or Unwilling for this task. Hana notes that while Michael excels technically, he hasn't yet demonstrated the ability or willingness to process and respond to feedback constructively in real time.

Can They Do It—Right Now? (Ability)

When we assess ability in Situational Leadership®, we're looking at current performance, not potential. Ability is demonstrated through three components: knowledge, experience, and skill.

Knowledge

*The follower knows how to perform the specific
task, through training or relevant education*

Experience

*They've done the task before (or have
related experience that applies)*

Skill

*They're doing the task now at a
sustained, acceptable level*

The core question here is, "Are they?" Are they currently performing at the level the task requires? Are they demonstrating knowledge, experience, and skill? We're not asking, "Could they?" If we're assigning them the task, we're assuming they're capable of performing the task at some point in the future.

A quick way to see the difference: Incoming freshmen at a prestigious university are admitted because of their potential, but their ability for college-level work isn't known until they actually start performing. It's the work they demonstrate, not the projections on their applications, that shows their true abilities.

And remember, this isn't a judgment of the person. It's simply an objective read on today's task. Being "unable" means the follower's knowledge, experience, or skill for this specific task isn't yet at a sustained, acceptable level.

The good news is ability grows. With practice, coaching, and aligned leadership in the next step, someone who's unable today may soon become fully functional and ready to perform. Step Two simply helps you pinpoint where they are so you can help them take the next step.

Ability is the easy part of the Performance Readiness® assessment because you, as the leader, have the final say on whether the follower is able. Even if the follower doesn't agree with your assessment, you're the one who defines what success looks like; it's a clear yes or no. To achieve alignment with the follower on their ability, you should be able to point to observable metrics that show where they're falling short.

Will They Do It? (Willingness)

Once you've considered whether someone can perform a task, the next question is whether they will. That's willingness—the confidence, commitment, and motivation a performer brings to a specific task.

Each component offers a different lens.

Confidence

*When the performer believes they **can do** the task. The individual believes they're capable of success. When confidence is low, you'll often see hesitation, tentative questions, or frequent requests for reassurance.*

Commitment

*When the performer **will do** the task. They make an effort because they care about the results. When commitment is low, you might see delays, reluctance, or disengagement.*

Motivation

*When the performer **wants to do** the task. They have a desire to put in the effort. Someone may have confidence and commitment but still lack motivation because of competing priorities, changing interests, or other circumstances.*

In practice it's difficult to distinguish between commitment and motivation because the behaviors often overlap. That's why Situational Leadership® combines them as commitment and motivation when assessing willingness.

When willingness is low, regardless of which component is driving it, you'll typically see predictable behaviors just described. Again, none of these reactions mean someone is unmotivated as a person. They simply reflect how they're experiencing this particular assignment. A performer may be highly motivated overall yet insecure about how to begin a particular assignment. In that case their strongest need is confidence, not desire.

That's often how willingness works: The strongest-felt need drives the response. And if we bring this back to Maslow's hierarchy from chapter 4, unwillingness or insecurity usually signals an unmet need. Maybe the person doesn't feel safe taking a risk, maybe their self-esteem has taken a hit, or maybe the task feels disconnected from their sense of purpose.

Here's a simple illustration. Imagine someone offers you $10 million to climb Mount Everest. Your motivation might be through the roof. But if you've never climbed before, you may be more concerned about surviving than about the reward. Even with strong motivation, lacking confidence would result in low willingness for this task. In other words context is key. Understanding which need is pulling the hardest equips you to address it in Step Three.

A Conversation with Your Follower

Figuring out your follower's ability and willingness doesn't have to be complicated. After you've clearly defined the task, just have a simple conversation. Ask your follower the following:

- "Have you done this task before?"
- "If so, where and when?"
- "How would you describe your skill or ability for this task right now?"

Next, get a sense for how enthusiastic they are about performing the task by asking the following:

- "Do you feel confident?"
- "Are you excited to jump in?"

- "Are other responsibilities making you cautious to take this task on, or is there another reason why you might be reluctant?"

How able and willing is your follower for this task today, on a scale of 1 to 5? You can probably find out with a few quick questions!

Willingness is often harder to assess than ability because it's intrinsic to the follower. Only the follower truly knows how they feel about a task, and often they obscure that truth for fear of judgment. This is why building trust is so important. This assessment becomes much easier if the follower can communicate their insecurity or unwillingness openly. In the absence of trust, you'll need to rely on keen behavioral observation to pick up on these cues.

How Ability and Willingness Work Together: The Decision Tree

Even though ability and willingness measure different things, they don't operate in isolation. Together, they determine a performer's Performance Readiness® for a specific task. In the Situational Leadership® framework, the two continually influence each other; a meaningful change in one usually affects the other.

For example, willingness can impact how well a person uses their current ability. High willingness can accelerate growth; low willingness can restrict it. Likewise, ability can strengthen or weaken willingness. As ability increases, confidence often increases with it; when ability lags, confidence and motivation may decline.

It's important not to confuse the two. In Argyris's immaturity-maturity theory, he identified that an individual can be more mature in one dimension than another. (In this case the dimensions are ability and willingness.) A person can be willing but not able. Someone may be enthusiastic about a task they've never done before yet lack the knowledge, experience, or skill to perform at a sustained, acceptable level. The reverse is also true: A person can be able but not willing. They may have demonstrated strong performance in the past but no longer feel motivated or committed to doing the task today.

Ability and willingness move together, shaping each other. Understanding how each contributes to a performer's current state helps leaders determine the most accurate readiness level and, in turn, how to respond.

So how do we translate this into practice? Situational Leadership® uses a simple decision path to help leaders assess current Performance Readiness®. After identifying the specific task, start by asking whether the person is currently performing it at a sustained, acceptable level. This yes/no question helps you gauge ability. If the answer is no, the performer will fall into either R1 or R2. If the answer is yes, they're somewhere in R3 or R4.

Next, consider willingness. Is the person demonstrating confidence, commitment, or motivation for the task today? If not, their readiness is either R1 or R3, depending on ability. If yes, they're either R2 or R4.

These two questions—*Can they do it? Will they do it?*—lead to the four Performance Readiness® Levels.

- **R1: Unable and Insecure or Unwilling**
- **R2: Unable but Confident or Willing**
- **R3: Able but Insecure or Unwilling**
- **R4: Able and Confident and Willing**

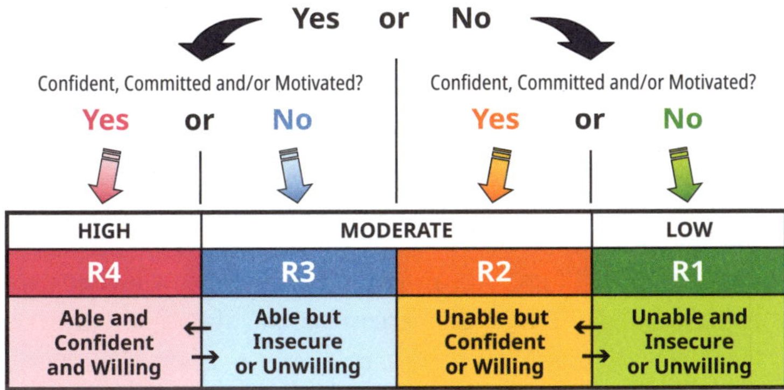

It's also important to note that Performance Readiness® is neutral. Where someone lands—whether R1, R2, R3, or R4—doesn't measure talent, character, or future potential. All of us could place ourselves at different points along the continuum depending on the specific task. Low readiness simply means someone needs more direction or support for the task to perform well. High readiness means they can act more independently for the task. Both are normal.

Readiness is also dynamic. People move up, down, and across levels depending on the task, changing responsibilities, personal factors, or organizational shifts. Someone might be R4 for one task and R1 for another, and that could change tomorrow. The point of Step Two is simply to understand what's true right now so you can respond to this moment.

The Dangers of Typecasting

We've emphasized again and again that Performance Readiness® and Situational Leadership® apply to a task. That's because typecasting is dangerous. It's easy to let unconscious biases—personality differences, performance on other tasks, tenure, and so on—lead you to assume that a high performer is automatically R4. Not just R4 for this task but R4 as a person. That small slip in language creates a big problem.

For the performer who's been typecast as an R4, you've just set expectations they can't possibly meet. No one is R4 for every task. And when they inevitably fall short, they'll feel frustrated and even resentful, believing their leader abandoned them.

Typecasting shows up at the other end of the continuum too. Remember, Situational Leaders must operate with a Theory Y mindset. When you typecast someone as a perpetual R1, you remove the possibility of growth. You lock yourself into a leader-driven approach regardless of the person's actual ability or willingness. It teaches them there's no reason to improve or excel because they'll never be trusted or given autonomy.

A Closer Look at the Four Readiness Levels

Step Two ultimately leads you to identify where the performer lands on the Performance Readiness® continuum. Now let's take a deeper look at them through the lens of diagnosis.

R1: Unable and Insecure or Unwilling

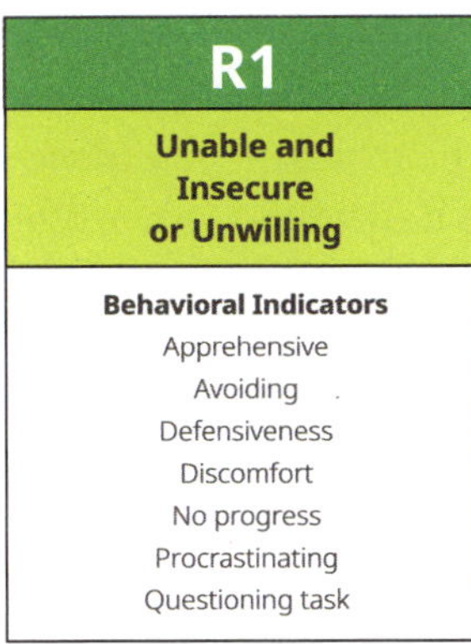

When someone is at R1 for a task, they're not yet demonstrating the knowledge, experience, or skill to perform that task at a sustained, acceptable level. Which means they're feeling unsure or hesitant about taking it on. That often shows up as apprehension, defensiveness, or avoidance. You may notice they're stalling, second-guessing themselves, or holding back altogether.

They might say things such as the following:

- "I don't think I'm the right person for this. What if I mess up?"
- "I'm just warning you . . . I probably can't do this."

R2: Unable but Confident or Willing

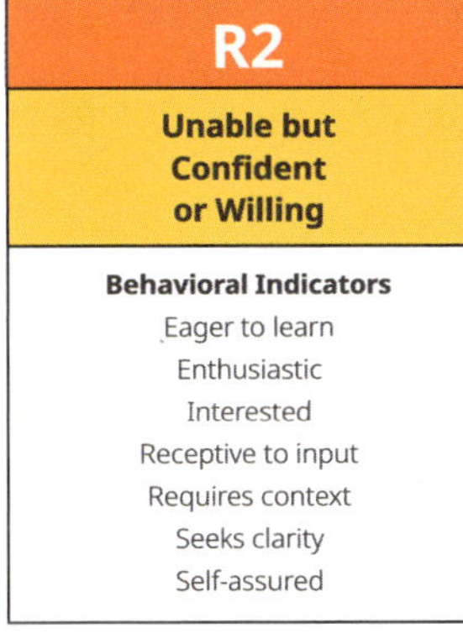

At R2, the performer doesn't yet have the demonstrated knowledge, experience, or skill to deliver the task consistently, but they want to. You'll often see enthusiasm, curiosity, and a genuine desire to dive in. They ask questions, look for context, and welcome feedback because they're eager to learn and get it right.

They might say things such as the following:

- "I was really excited to try out some new ideas on this task, but I'm new and open to your feedback!"
- "I've always wanted to learn how to do this—this is exciting!"

R3: Able but Insecure or Unwilling

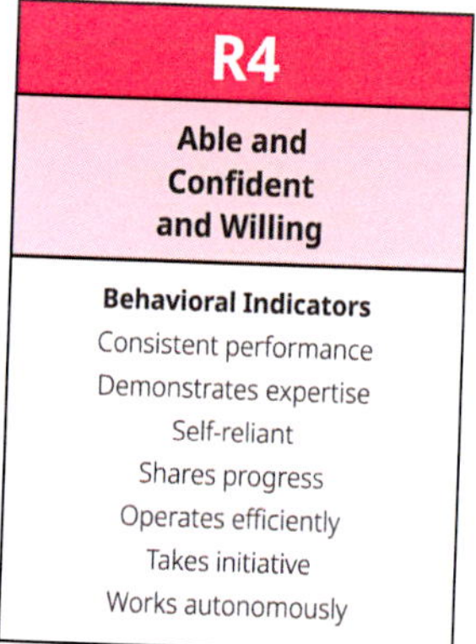

At R3, the performer has the knowledge, experience, and skill to do the task at a sustained, acceptable level, but something is holding them back. If confidence is low, you'll see hesitation, anxiety, or frequent check-ins as they look for reassurance. If motivation is low, you may notice resistance, frustration, or a lack of follow-through, even though they're fully capable.

They might say things such as the following:

- "I'm still not sure I'm ready."
- "I've done this so many times . . . why do I have to do it again?"

R4: Able and Confident and Willing

At R4, the performer has mastered the task. They have the knowledge, experience, and skill, and they bring the confidence, commitment, and motivation to run with it. They take ownership, work independently, and keep others informed along the way. You'll notice this level of readiness in their initiative, efficiency, and proactive problem-solving.

They might say things such as the following:

- "I truly enjoy moving this project forward on my own."
- "I've identified a problem, and I have a few ideas for solutions I'd like to recommend to the team."

The 70/40 Rule

Gut instinct isn't the most reliable path to an accurate diagnosis. But overanalyzing can stall progress just as quickly. How do you know when you have enough information to move forward?

Former Secretary of State and Chairman of the Joint Chiefs of Staff Colin Powell offered a helpful guideline: Never make a decision with less than 40 percent of the information—but don't wait until you have more than 70 percent.[3] Less than 40 percent and you're guessing. More than 70 percent and you've likely missed your window to act.

In other words don't get stuck in analysis paralysis. Once you've gathered about 70 percent of the information, it's time to make a move!

Always Assess, Never Assume

So much of leadership happens in the quiet work of diagnosing. Step One helps you get clear on what the work really is. Step Two helps you understand where the performer is today in relation to that work. Together, these steps make it possible to choose the right leadership style in response.

When we skip diagnosis, we skip understanding. And when we skip understanding, we lead on assumption, often with disappointing results. But when we discipline ourselves to slow down just enough to define the task and assess readiness, we see our people more accurately. We uncover what they need, not what we *assume* they need. And most importantly, we position them, and ourselves, for success.

Let's circle back to Hana and Michael.

Step One helped Hana separate Michael's work into distinct

components. Step Two helped her assess his Performance Readiness®
for each one. And that assessment revealed that Michael sits at different
readiness levels based on the different tasks—a truth you'll see show
up over and over again as you apply this model.

For the main build-the-app responsibility, Michael shows strong
willingness and relevant experience. The scope is larger than he's
handled before, and it requires more alignment across functions,
so Hana places him at R2. He's eager and capable of learning, but he
hasn't yet demonstrated the ability to perform this level of work at a
sustained, acceptable level.

For the second task of receiving and responding to feedback in the
moment, Hana sees something different. Based on the behaviors she
observed during the recent stakeholder meeting, Michael is showing R1.
He struggles to adjust in real time, disengages when others influence the
direction, and demonstrates low willingness for this aspect of the work.

This is why taking the time to diagnose *for each task* is so critical.
If Hana assumed Michael's strong technical ability meant he was
equally ready to receive feedback in real time, she would misread
what he needs next. Instead, she's able to name, task by task, where
he's at. That clarity will help her create alignment, and alignment is
what makes adaptive leadership possible.

Now that Hana understands the tasks and has assessed Michael's
current readiness levels, she's ready for Step Three: choosing the
appropriate leadership response. That's where we're headed next.

The Second Core Leadership Skill: Adapting

Adapting is the ability to adjust your leadership style to fit the
needs of others.

It's the bridge between Step Two and Step Three of the Situational
Leadership® process.

Once you understand a performer's readiness, you adapt. You
shift your approach and communicate the leadership style match.

Chapter 6 Review

Here are the key takeaways from chapter 6:

- Step Two (Assess Current Performance Readiness®) is about diagnosing where the performer is today in relation to a specific task.
- Performance Readiness® is made up of two components: ability (knowledge, experience, skill) and willingness (confidence, commitment, motivation).
- Leaders must rely on observable behavior, not assumptions.
- Ability answers the question, Can they do it right now? Willingness answers the question, Will they do it right now?
- These two questions lead to the four Performance Readiness® Levels.
    - R1 (Unable and Insecure or Unwilling), R2 (Unable but Confident or Willing),
    - R3 (Able but Insecure or Unwilling), and R4 (Able and Confident and Willing).
- Performance Readiness® is task-specific and dynamic. A performer can be R4 for one part of a role and R1 for another.
- Accurate diagnosis sets the stage for every leadership move that follows. When leaders assess readiness well, they know exactly what the performer needs next.

Reflect and Apply

Before you move on, take a moment to reflect on how this chapter applies to your leadership today.

1. Think of a specific task. Based on what you've observed—not what you assume—how would you rate your performer's ability and willingness today?
2. What behaviors signal their current Performance Readiness® Level? What cues have you possibly overlooked?

3.   Where might your follower see themself differently than you see them—and how can you open a conversation to clarify readiness together?

Flex and Adapt

Step Three: Match and Communicate Leader Response

Hana and Michael sit down for their weekly one-one-one a few days after the tension-filled team meeting. Normally, these conversations are easy for her. Hana's natural rhythm as a leader is all about dialogue, asking good questions, drawing people out, and helping them think through problems on their own. That approach has always worked well with Michael. But today is different.

She watched his excitement about the new app turn into defensiveness the moment feedback entered the room. If she walks into this conversation relying only on her usual collaborative style, she knows she'll miss the opportunity to help Michael grow. Michael doesn't need a brainstorming partner today; he needs some steady guardrails to help him move forward.

So she sketches out a simple plan of attack for the conversation: Start with the topic he's most energized about (the app itself) so he feels grounded and supported. Then shift, gently but firmly, into a conversation about how he handled feedback in the meeting.

"Okay," Hana begins, "let's start with the app."

Michael lights up immediately. "I've been thinking about it

nonstop," he says. "The new environment, the mobile deployment—I'm excited to wrap my head around all of it."

Hana smiles. This is exactly why she pushed for him to lead the project. "It's a great opportunity," she says. "This week I need you to revise the outline based on the stakeholder feedback and build version 1.2 before next week's check-in."

Michael pauses. "Wait. Why do I need to show my work every week in the meeting? I've never had to do that before."

Hana resists the urge to soften or overexplain and instead gives him the detailed reasoning he actually needs and explains the why behind the ask.

"Because of the size of this project," she says, "we've got more cross-functional partners involved. Everyone in that room needs visibility. Showing your weekly progress isn't about checking your work. It's about the rest of the team understanding what we're building so they can support it."

"Okay, got it," he says, jotting down a few notes.

Then Hana shifts the conversation.

"Michael, I also want to talk about the meeting last week," she says. "Can I share a couple of things I noticed?"

He tenses but nods.

"When people started giving you feedback and sharing thoughts, I noticed you push your chair back and turn away from the team. And you stopped taking notes the moment Donald shared his idea."

Michael's face flushes. "I know. I just . . . I have such a clear picture of where this project should go. Everyone's comments felt overwhelming. And honestly, none of them are developers."

Hana understands, and she also knows this is the moment for directness, not sugarcoating.

"I hear you," she says. "But everyone's ideas contribute to the success of this launch. So here's what I need from you next time: Share your updates, then stay quiet and take notes while everyone else talks. Let your body language show you're engaged—eye contact, open posture, nodding, and note-taking. Can you do that?"

He exhales. "Yeah. You're right."

She softens, her natural leadership style peeking through as she asks, "Are you okay?"

He nods.

She then adds, "Michael, I want you to know that I still believe you're the right person to lead this work, but leading this work includes using your technical expertise to help other key stakeholders feel a sense of ownership and excitement about what we're doing. When we're in the next meeting, I'll look for you to express these collaborative behaviors."

"Message received," Michael says as the meeting draws to a close.

Notice in that one meeting, Hana is able to adapt her leadership style twice. First, she gives Michael the encouragement and clarity he needs to stay on track with the app; then she offers direct expectations around how he receives and responds to feedback. She doesn't change who she is. She simply meets him where he is for each task.

That's what this next step in the Situational Leadership® Model is all about. In the pages ahead, we'll break down exactly how to match your leadership approach to a performer's ability and willingness, how to bring the right balance of relational and task behavior, and how to communicate in a way that aligns with what your follower needs.

Consistent *and* Flexible

Two words often used to describe great leaders: consistent and flexible.

Consistency

Showing up with steadiness and fairness. People want to know what to expect from you—where they stand, what success looks like, and how you'll respond. This creates psychological safety and trust and an environment where people can show up as their best selves.

Flexibility

Showing up with agility and awareness. People want a leader who meets them where they are, someone who responds to what's needed in the moment. This creates growth, momentum, and an environment where people can build confidence and skill.

Both qualities are essential. Who doesn't want a leader who sets high standards, tells the truth, gives fair feedback, and recognizes effort and results?

But here's the paradox: The most inconsistent thing a leader can do is treat everyone the same.

It simply doesn't work.

When someone doesn't know what to do, they need guidance. When they've mastered a task, they need autonomy. When they're struggling, they need support and space to think. It all depends on the task and the follower's readiness to perform it. That's where Step Three comes into play: adapting your leadership style to match the diagnosis.

To do that well, leaders start with self-awareness. Earlier in the book, you were invited to reflect on which leadership styles come most naturally to you and which ones push you out of your comfort zone. This is very common. Most leaders have a style that feels instinctive and easy, while others can feel forced or uncomfortable.

> **" The most inconsistent thing a leader can do is treat everyone the same.**

The Best Style Is the One That Fits

Our LEAD Assessment gives leaders insight into their most frequently used style, their mismatches, and their adaptability. Take this condensed version of our LEAD Assessment to get a better understanding of your leadership as we dig into Step Three.

LEAD survey data shows that as participative leadership becomes more common, leaders are more often missing the mark when their people need explicit clarity and direction. There's no single "best" leadership style, only the one that fits the situation and the follower's needs.

We see this all the time in workshops. A leader will say, "Ahh . . . now I see why that one-on-one felt so awkward. Andrew was brand new to the software, and my 'You've got this' didn't match what he actually needed at that time."

Leaders who cling to a preferred style limit themselves. Leaders who can adapt and meet people where they are, based on the task, unlock performance and growth.

Awareness is just the beginning. Real development happens when you intentionally practice leadership styles that don't come naturally. The most effective leaders can use any leadership style when the situation calls for it, not just the one that feels most comfortable.

Flexibility
The ability to use all four leadership styles

Adaptability
The ability to use the right style at the right time

In the words of Hersey, "Being an effective leader is a function of using the 'right style' at the 'right time.'" Up to this point, you've clarified the task and diagnosed the performer's readiness. Now it's time to translate that diagnosis into action by selecting and communicating the leadership approach that aligns with what the performer needs most.

> **" *Being an effective leader is a function of using the 'right style' at the 'right time.'***

This is where the Situational Leadership® Model removes all the guesswork. Instead of relying on habit, leaders are equipped with four leadership styles, each blending task and relationship behaviors in different ways. These styles allow leaders to meet performers where they are for the specific task.

Before we put this into practice, let's revisit the foundation—the task and relationship behaviors that form every Situational Leadership® response and how those behaviors combine into four distinct leadership styles.

A Deeper Dive into the Styles

Previously we introduced the two core dimensions that shape every Situational Leadership® response: task behavior and relationship behavior. Before we match styles in Step Three, let's ground ourselves in what these two behaviors entail.

Task behavior (or directive behavior) reflects the extent to which a leader defines roles and structures activities. It can range from low to high and typically includes the following:

- Providing clear direction and structure
- Establishing goals, priorities, and timelines
- Monitoring progress and offering corrective guidance

Relationship behavior (or supportive behavior) reflects the extent to which a leader engages in two-way communication and active listening. It also ranges from low to high and generally includes the following:

- Inviting dialogue and feedback
- Facilitating collaboration and actively listening
- Providing reassurance, recognition, and encouragement

Now that you understand that these behaviors originated in early autocratic and democratic leadership theories, we can take a look at how they function inside the Situational Leadership® Model. These two dimensions intersect to form four leadership styles (S1–S4). Here's how task and relationship behaviors combine into four distinct leadership styles:

Style 1 (S1): Telling, Directing, Guiding

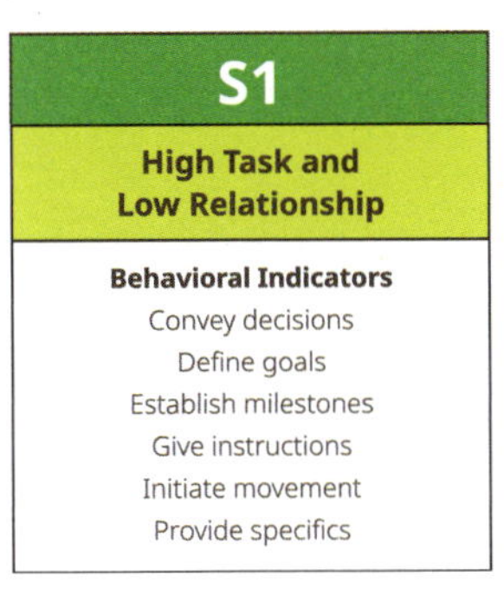

High Task, Low Relationship

You saw a glimpse of S1 earlier when Hana shifted into a more directive approach with Michael, giving clear expectations and specific next steps when he needed more guidance.

S1 provides explicit direction and structure to get things moving. But here's an important nuance: One leader's S1 might look different from another's. Even though S1 is always high task and low relationship, leaders can personalize how they express it.

For example, both "telling" and "guiding" fall under S1 behaviors. One leader might say, "I'd never tell someone what to do," yet feel completely comfortable guiding someone step-by-step. Another might lean naturally toward directing or instructing. It doesn't matter which word you choose; it matters that the performer gets the clarity, specificity, and support they need to be successful.

What S1 Sounds Like

- Conveying decisions: "For the Polish translations project, we're going to check the edits sent by the client, send them to our vendor for native speaker review, then review internally before deciding on next steps."

- Establishing milestones: "On project CX128, we'll pilot in Q1 2026, post edits by April, then move on to round two before the next pilot in Q3."
- Giving instructions: "When you arrive in the parking lot, go to the right side of the building, and you'll see a parking deck. Go up to the third level and access the elevator so you can enter through the main lobby. Sharon will meet you there and walk you to the training room."

Style 2 (S2): Selling, Persuading, Explaining

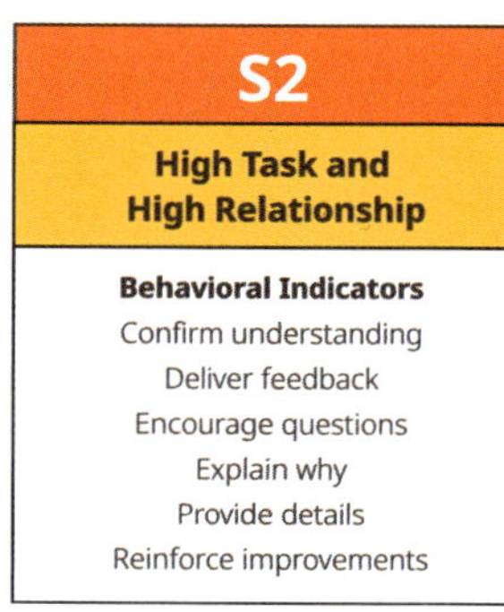

High Task, High Relationship

S2 combines direction with dialogue, explanation, and encouragement. The performer still needs structure, but they also benefit from context, conversation, and reinforcement as they build capability and confidence.

This is the kind of approach Hana used in the first part of her one-on-one with Michael. She focused on reinforcing his excitement while still laying out the expectations and guardrails he needed for a task that was new to him.

What S2 Sounds Like

- Confirm understanding: "Natalie, I want to confirm your understanding on utilizing the CRM to enter call notes after each client session."
- Explain why: "The reason our team is sunsetting the 2012 product line is due to outdated examples and workplace norms that no longer reflect our audience."

- Reinforce improvement: "You asked wonderful questions in the last meeting—thank you. Next week, please continue to ask those questions but during the Q and A portion at the end of the call."

Style 3 (S3): Participating, Problem-Solving, Encouraging

<table>
<tr><td colspan="2">S3</td></tr>
<tr><td colspan="2">High Relationship and Low Task</td></tr>
<tr><td colspan="2">Behavioral Indicators
Build confidence
Compliment performance
Discuss apprehension
Enable next steps
Solicit input
Synthesize concerns</td></tr>
</table>

High Relationship, Low Task

S3 provides collaboration and encouragement that help the performer take ownership. The performer is in a challenging spot here, as they struggle with either confidence or commitment/motivation. The leader needs to support them in getting to the other side of this on the merits of their proven ability.

The good news is that our LEAD data consistently shows R3/S3 as the most common match between leaders and followers. In other words leaders are generally getting this right, providing R3 performers with the support they need.

What S3 Sounds Like

- Build confidence: "Alex, you've built compelling ads all season, and this time will be no different. What are your initial thoughts on this one?"
- Discuss apprehension: "What's concerning you about the upcoming conference? I want to hear more about your hesitation."
- Solicit input: "Given your resistance, tell me what next steps you'd take to ensure the presentation is successful next week."

Style 4 (S4): Delegating, Monitoring, Observing

S4

Low Relationship and Low Task

Behavioral Indicators

Encourage autonomy
Eliminate barriers
Entrust decision-making
Remain accessible
Resist overloading
Track progress

Low Task, Low Relationship

S4 is all about giving the performer autonomy while staying available as needed. In Stogdill's research this closely aligned with what he called laissez-faire leadership, a style characterized by stepping back once the performer demonstrates strong ability and commitment. But low relationship behavior doesn't mean *no* relationship behavior. You still remain accessible for check-ins and to remove obstacles as they arise.

What S4 Sounds Like

- Encourage autonomy: "I know you're an expert when it comes to managing the account, so keep doing what you're doing."
- Entrust decision-making: "I trust you on this. Please go ahead and make decisions on next steps."
- Remain accessible: "I want you to feel empowered to lead this project, and I'm always here if you need support."

Remember, no single style is universally "better." Each can be effective when matched to the performer's Performance Readiness® for the task.

As we've established, Performance Readiness® is dynamic. As someone learns, gains confidence, struggles, or stretches into something new, their needs change. That means your leadership must change with them. The goal isn't to stick with one favorite style or to lead only in ways that feel natural. Effective leaders stretch. They adapt. They deliver the style that best enables success, even if it's not their default.

Situational Leadership®
Influence Behaviors

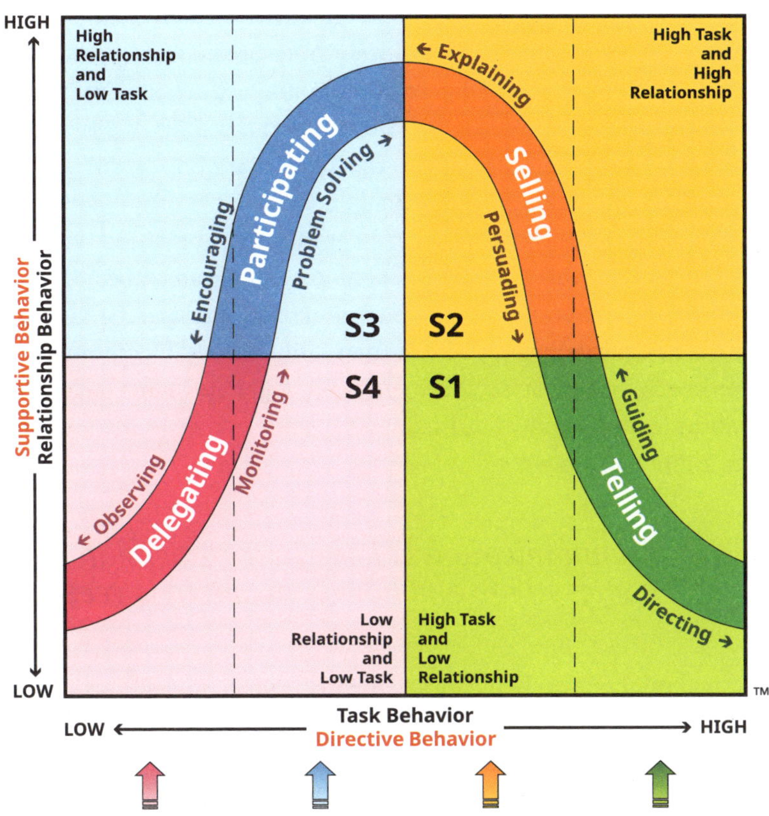

Performance Readiness®

Communicate with Intention

Adaptability allows leaders to recognize the right response, and communication is what makes that response effective. Without clear communication, effective leadership can't occur. Yet a recent *Harvard Business Review* study found that 69 percent of managers are uncomfortable communicating.[4] If more leaders understood the skills of Situational Leadership®, they'd feel far more confident communicating in ways that match what their people actually need.

The challenge is that effective communication shifts with the situation. What works perfectly in one conversation can completely backfire in another. But when you understand the specific task and a performer's readiness, you can then tailor how you communicate accordingly—what you say, how you say it, and how often you engage. Communication is how your leadership style comes to life and how your intent is received.

> **"** *Communication is how your leadership style comes to life and how your intent is received.*

That might mean being direct and decisive in one interaction and slowing down to listen and draw others out in the next. Great communicators flex their approach, choosing words, tone, and timing that fit the person and the situation.

If you're a naturally participative leader, using a directive style might feel uncomfortable, maybe even *wrong*. You might think, *There's no way I'm going to tell someone what to do.* But when direction is what a performer needs to succeed, as Brené Brown coined, "Clear is kind."

Conversely, if you tend to be more direct, stepping back to ask questions might feel unnatural. You might worry, *If I'm not leading the discussion, I'm not leading at all.* But when you control every conversation, you leave no room for others to think or contribute.

The Third Core Leadership Skill: Communicating

Communicating is the ability to translate your intent so others can receive it, and it's one of the core competencies needed to be successful in Step Three. Because communication in leadership isn't one size fits all, it requires understanding the situation, choosing your tone, and delivering your message in a way that builds trust and alignment.

When leaders communicate well, they speak differently to different people (without losing authenticity), ensuring the message lands the way they intend.

The truth is, effective communication requires range. The goal isn't to change who you are; it's to translate your intent in a way others can receive. Instead of thinking, *I have to tell someone what to do*, reframe it as, *I'm providing clear direction to help them succeed.* Instead of thinking, *I'm losing control of the discussion*, reframe it as, *I'm creating space for others to contribute.*

Now let's see what this looks like in practice. In the following scenarios, we'll watch Priya, a nonprofit department manager, adapt and communicate with her team—Alex, Jada, Malik, and Taylor—each representing a different Performance Readiness® Level. Together, these examples illustrate all four leadership styles in action, showing how the right mix of adaptability and communication can unlock confidence, growth, and results.

S1: Create Movement

Alex has just joined the nonprofit and is tackling a task he's never done before: compiling his first quarterly impact report for one of the organization's community programs. He's bright and eager, but the reporting platform and process are unfamiliar. Even though he wants to do well, it's clear he feels uncertain about where to begin.

His manager, Priya, recognizes immediately that Alex is at R1—low ability and uncertain willingness for this task. So Priya steps in and takes the lead. She explains the assignment from the top: Here's the goal. Here's what the final report should include. Here's exactly where to find the information.

Then she breaks down the workflow step-by-step: where to pull data, how to format the report, and how to submit it for review. She sets clear expectations for what needs to be completed, when it's due, and what "good" looks like.

Priya keeps the conversation focused and straightforward. Most of her questions are closed-ended, with the goal of confirming understanding: "Does this part make sense?" "Do you see where this data lives?" "Can you try running that section now?" Alex can't handle open brainstorming or autonomy yet. He needs guidance, for someone to clearly light the way.

When someone in Alex's position doesn't get that kind of structure for a task they've never done before, their insecurity only heightens. They may dive in and take uninformed action in an effort to show initiative, but the chances of that action producing the right results are really low. Over time this only leads to growing frustration, often ending with the thought, *I really wish somebody had been here to tell me what to do.* S1 prevents that spiral by offering the direction and specificity the inexperienced performer needs.

So in this case, Priya focuses on defining milestones, explaining the process, and making immediate decisions. Even though the style is leader-driven, Priya isn't cold or disconnected. She's still present, attentive, and encouraging. She offers reinforcement for small wins along the way: "Yep, that's the right format. Keep going." But the emphasis remains on direction and supervision.

S1 helps Alex move from "I've never done this before" to "Okay, I can handle the next step."

That's what S1 is all about: creating movement and getting someone going. It combines high task and low relationship behaviors—telling, guiding, directing, instructing—to develop the follower's Performance Readiness®. Communication flows from leader to performer and focuses on specific direction and close supervision to create early progress and begin development.

S2: Leverage Enthusiasm

Jada has been with the nonprofit for a few months, and today she's taking on her first donor presentation for a community funding campaign. She's never presented to donors before, but she's excited. She's reviewed past slide decks, watched recordings from previous events, and even drafted her own outline.

Priya recognizes that Jada is at R2: low ability but high willingness for this task. She has energy and commitment; she just needs experience and structure. So Priya leans into S2.

She starts by clarifying the outcome (what success looks like) and gives Jada the key talking points and flow of the presentation. She outlines timing, audience expectations, and the logistics of who's covering what. But unlike S1, Priya doesn't stop at direction. She opens the conversation up: "What questions do you have?" "What parts feel unclear?" "How would you describe our mission in your own words?"

When someone approaches a new task with Jada's level of enthusiasm but doesn't receive the reinforcement and direction they need, it slows their development. Her questions deserve answers, and her excitement needs to be acknowledged, but Priya also has to keep the decision-making and feedback in place until Jada has a few presentations under her belt and can rely on her own experience.

They talk through the why behind each section: why certain stories resonate most with donors, why one visual works better than another, why specific timing is important. When Jada hesitates, Priya coaches: "Here's how I'd frame that . . . Try this."

There's still structure from the leader. Priya sets the expectations, timelines, and nonnegotiables. But there's also space to ask questions, to interpret, to practice out loud. They rehearse together. Priya provides feedback and encourages Jada to try again, adjusting transitions and tone. Her questions are two way and open-ended: "How did that feel?" "What would you tweak?" "What part feels most natural to you?"

As they work together, Jada grows even more confident. She understands not only what to say but why she needs to say it. She begins to make the message her own. Priya reinforces her progress as she builds skill: "Your energy here is great—keep that. And your closing story landed perfectly that time."

S2 leverages Jada's enthusiasm to help her develop experience. She's still not ready to run solo, but she's learning in dialogue, and the coaching helps her take ownership. Jada leaves their time together thinking, *I can do this. I know what's expected, and I understand why.*

S2 blends high task and high relationship behaviors, providing detail and leader-driven decisions while also encouraging questions, explaining the why, and tapping into motivation. The purpose of S2 is to leverage enthusiasm while still providing the clarity and guardrails the follower needs to be successful. Communication flows both ways, with the goal of increasing the performer's skill and readiness for the task.

S3: Explore Alternatives

Malik has managed community partnerships for several years. He knows the organization's programs, the key stakeholders, and the process for building local collaborations. He's fully capable of performing the task, but this new partnership feels tricky because the other organization is large, bureaucratic, and slow to move. Malik's confidence has taken a hit, and he's second-guessing decisions he used to make easily.

Priya notices the shift and recognizes that Malik is at R3: high ability but variable willingness for this task. He can do the work; right now, he just doesn't believe he can.

So Priya leans into S3.

She invites Malik into a conversation: "Talk me through what feels off right now."

Malik shares his concerns about the partner's expectations, a change in leadership, and a few setbacks that made him feel like the project is struggling. Instead of telling him what to do, Priya listens actively. She asks thoughtful, open-ended questions: "What options have you considered?" "What's worked for you in similar partnerships?" "Where do you feel stuck?"

In doing so she avoids the temptation to jump in and start solving

Malik's problems, to offer solutions from her own experience just to help him out. A noble motive but not one that serves him well in the long run. If Priya went down that path, Malik would be implementing her solutions, not his. So instead, they begin problem-solving together. Malik identifies two possible paths; Priya reflects them back and helps him think through the pros and cons. She reminds him of past successes and highlights the strengths he's shown in navigating complex relationships.

"You managed that regional collaboration last year—that was just as challenging, and you brought everyone together. What worked for you then?"

As they talk, Malik reconnects with his strengths. His confidence starts to return. Priya encourages him to decide how he wants to move forward. He chooses a path, and she supports it. She doesn't make the call; Malik owns the decision.

Throughout the conversation Priya keeps task direction light. She's not telling him what to do step-by-step; he doesn't need that. What he needs is space to process, encouragement to trust his experience, and a partner to help him recenter. As he wraps up the conversation, Malik says, "Okay. I've got this."

The purpose of S3 is to explore alternatives that help the individual regain confidence and take ownership of the next steps. Whether participating, encouraging, problem-solving, or facilitating, S3 aims to help the individual rebuild confidence and motivation. With low task and high relationship behaviors, the leader creates space for two-way dialogue and performer-led decisions, offering support and partnership while the performer decides the path forward.

S4: Enable Mastery

Taylor has been leading program launches for years. She's skilled, confident, and consistently delivers strong results. When a new initiative is added to the organization's strategic plan, she immediately starts drafting her proposal. She outlines goals, identifies partners, and maps timelines. She clearly knows the work and is ready to run with it.

Priya recognizes that Taylor is at R4: high ability and high willingness for this task. She doesn't need direction, coaching, or problem-solving; she needs *space*.

So Priya leans into S4. She communicates the shift clearly to Taylor, letting her know that she's ready to take full ownership of the project and that Priya trusts her judgment. Then she turns responsibility for both decisions and implementation over to her. Taylor determines the approach, timelines, and next steps. She reaches out when she needs a resource or wants to test an idea, but otherwise, she's in the driver's seat.

The flow of communication now runs from Taylor to Priya. Taylor keeps her updated at key checkpoints, sharing progress, flagging risks, and noting any support she might need. Priya stays informed, but she isn't steering. Her focus is simply to remove barriers and ensure Taylor has what she needs to stay successful. Because she trusts her expertise on the task, Priya doesn't jump in or overload her with extra work. She monitors progress from a distance but remains available if Taylor hits a snag.

This is where S4 can become challenging for many leaders. When they aren't actively directing, coaching, or correcting, it can feel like they're not adding value. But for someone at R4, stepping back *is* the value add. High performers need room to perform. Overleading them doesn't accelerate results; it erodes commitment and motivation. Gallup's research underscores this: People don't leave companies; they leave managers.[5] And when top performers leave, they're typically in search of increased freedom to do what they do best. (And mind you, the gap they leave behind is rarely quick or easy to fill.)

Priya adapts by stepping back, communicating trust through intentional restraint. That space empowers Taylor to take full ownership of her work, and Taylor thrives. The task is familiar, she's confident in her skill, and she has the freedom to make decisions and move quickly. She feels respected and accountable.

S4 blends low task and low relationship behaviors—delegating, observing, monitoring, empowering—to help highly capable and confident performers continue to master their work. Autonomy is the default; support is offered only when needed to enable mastery.

Even though we don't know what Priya's natural leadership tendencies might be, we can see her flexing to give each team member exactly what they need, based on their ability and willingness, to move forward and grow. That's the essence of Situational Leadership®: meeting people where they are so they can build confidence, develop proficiency, and be successful.

When leaders get it right, when their style matches a performer's readiness, the impact is immediate. You'll see progress, confidence, and ownership grow before your eyes. But when the match is off, things feel much different. That's what we'll look at next—the cost of a mismatch and what happens when a leader's approach doesn't align with what the performer truly needs.

Overleading

Even experienced leaders can miss the mark when it comes to matching their style to a follower's readiness. Here's how to recognize when you might be doing too much.

You're overleading when a follower reacts with frustration or impatience, when they rush your directions or say, "I've got it." This often comes from a leader's fear of letting go.

Try easing up by giving the follower more ownership, starting with lower-impact tasks. Set clear expectations for updates, then step back and trust them to deliver.

If you catch yourself overleading, pause and adjust.

"I'm giving you too much direction. What ideas do you have?"

Here are some cues you can look for in the moment to spot if you are overleading:

- You're doing all the talking, and the performer doesn't have any questions.
- The performer shows up more prepared than you expected.
- They try to wrap up the conversation quickly.
- You're initiating frequent touchpoints even though performance has been solid.
- The performer seems closed off or frustrated.

Underleading

Underleading is harder to spot. Followers may hesitate to ask for help, not wanting to disappoint you. You'll notice it when they ask repeated questions, seem stuck, or deliver poor results after long delays.

When that happens, step in with clarity and structure.

"I don't think I've given you enough direction. Let's walk through this together."

Your natural leadership style can influence which direction you tend to lean. If your default is S1 or S2—styles on the right side of the model—you're more likely to overlead. If your natural style leans toward S3 or S4, you're more likely to underlead. And remember, even if someone is highly capable (R4), using an S3 approach can still feel like overload.

Here's some cues you can look for in the moment that might indicate you are underleading:

- The performer asks unexpected questions.
- Their performance isn't meeting the standard you expected.
- They're reaching out to other team members for support without your prompting.
- They keep asking for more specifics.
- The follower seems anxious or nervous.

Our LEAD data shows that over time, leaders have become less likely to overlead but more likely to underlead or have a balanced approach. We attribute this shift to the change in workplace culture as organizations flatten and collaboration is emphasized. But it's important to remember that there are still times when you will need to use leader-driven styles.

When You Miss the Match

Performance Readiness® / Leadership Style Matrix

	R4	R3	R2	R1
S4	**MATCH** Delegating Observing Monitoring	**UNDERLEADING** Uninterested Withdrawing Uncaring	**UNDERLEADING** Disengaged Dumping Inaccessible	**UNDERLEADING** Ignoring Abandoning Uninvolved
S3	**OVERLEADING** Undertrusting Patronizing Not Letting Go	**MATCH** Participating Encouraging Problem Solving	**UNDERLEADING** Inflated Expectations Pacifying Nonspecific	**UNDERLEADING** Wavering Stalling Unearned Praise
S2	**OVERLEADING** Deceiving Defending Stifling Initiative	**OVERLEADING** Fixing Preaching Hindering Growth	**MATCH** Selling Explaining Persuading	**UNDERLEADING** Overexplaining Rationalizing Rewarding Nonperformance
S1	**OVERLEADING** Attacking Dominating Demotivating	**OVERLEADING** Reinforces Insecurity Controlling Demeaning	**OVERLEADING** Reduces Enthusiasm Demanding Creates Dependency	**MATCH** Telling Guiding Directing

In the earlier examples, we saw what happens when leadership style and Performance Readiness® align. But what about when they don't? When a leader utilizes the wrong style for the situation and the individual's current Performance Readiness®, that's a mismatch. Every mismatch tells a story, usually one of good intentions gone wrong, or a leader simply repeating what they've experienced from previous managers or the culture of their organization. The leader is trying to help, but the performer needs something different. The result is confusion, frustration, or stalled growth on both sides. Let's take a closer look at a few common mismatches and what they sound and feel like in real life.

R1/S3 Mismatch

An R1/S3 mismatch typically happens when a leader uses a participative approach with someone who has no experience and is trying to hide it. In other words the follower needs clarity, direction, and structure, but the leader provides empathy, listening, and collaboration instead.

At first this might sound supportive—the leader's being kind, encouraging, and conversational. But from the performer's perspective, it can come across as patronizing or condescending. The leader is trying to build confidence through discussion, but the follower's insecurity is heightened because they don't have the experience to engage.

Because the leader isn't providing the structure that's needed, the performer's ability doesn't develop, and willingness often drops even further. The result? Both leader and follower end up frustrated.

R2/S4 Mismatch

In this case the performer has energy and is excited about the task, but they don't yet have the skill or experience to do it well. The problem comes when the leader mistakes that excitement and enthusiasm for ability.

From the outside it might look like empowerment. The leader gives the performer full ownership, expecting them to "take it and run." But instead of running, the performer stalls out or makes mistakes they don't yet know how to correct.

This mismatch often results in a loss of trust on both sides. The performer's ability doesn't progress, and their willingness starts to slip as their confidence turns into self-doubt. The leader, meanwhile, is disappointed by the lack of results and unsure where things went wrong.

R3/S1 Mismatch

This mismatch happens when a leader continues to direct a follower who's developed task-related skills.

In this situation the performer is beginning to grow, develop, and demonstrate proficiency. At the same time, they lack the confidence necessary to take the next step and perform on their own. They might come into the conversation voicing that insecurity, which the leader misreads as a cry for help. As a result, the leader piles on structure, direction, and control, micromanaging every step.

When a capable person feels oversupervised, their motivation and morale drop fast. Confidence erodes. Some may freeze up, second-guess themselves, or even perform the task incorrectly—not because they don't know what they're doing but because they've lost ownership. Over time the performer's willingness declines, and their readiness can actually move *backward*.

The leader, meanwhile, starts convincing themselves that this follower can only perform if they stay close.

R4/S2

This mismatch happens when a leader can't stop coaching or hand over decision-making rights, even to the most proven performers. In this case the performer already knows what they're doing and what they're good at. But instead of giving them space and trust, the leader leans in with lots of direction, detailed guidance, and unnecessary check-ins.

What the leader sees as support, the performer experiences as control. The leader's tone can come across as preachy or even manipulative, and the performer quickly becomes both irritated and annoyed.

Even though the leader's intentions are good, the result is anything but. The performer's motivation drops, and resentment starts to build. Over time they may disengage or stop openly communicating, feeling that their competence isn't recognized or valued.

Meanwhile, the leader starts to feel uneasy with the performer's independence and tries to reassert control, creating a loop of frustration for both sides.

In 2025 Training Industry conducted an analysis of our LEAD data to uncover key insights and track how leadership trends have shifted over time. Here's what the data revealed:

- From 2009 to 2024, leaders have become less likely to over-lead but more likely to underlead.
- S3 has been the most common leadership style since 2015, peaking just before the pandemic. After 2020 there was a noticeable rise in S1 as a primary style.
- S1 leaders are most likely to make R2/S3 and R3/S2 mismatches.
- S2 leaders are most likely to make R1/S2 mismatches.
- S3 leaders are most likely to make R1/S2 and R2/S3 mismatches.
- S4 leaders are most likely to make R2/S3 and R1/S2 mismatches.
- Leaders with high adaptability scores are more likely to use all four styles evenly and effectively.

Leading Through Influence

At the top of the Situational Leadership® Model, you'll see the phrase "Influence Behaviors." It's there because every leadership style—S1 through S4—is fundamentally an expression of influence.

As you know from chapter 1, that influence is made possible by leveraging the three power bases—legitimate, expert, and referent power—each of which can be used to support every leadership style. Even if styles appear different on the surface, they share the same purpose of positively influencing another person's behavior so they can succeed.

Your leadership style isn't a preference or a personality; *it's your influence strategy*. When you choose high task behavior, you're influencing through clarity, structure, and direction. When you choose high relationship behavior, you're influencing through encouragement, dialogue, and support. When you pull back and empower, you're influencing through trust. Every choice flows from a single question: *What influence does this person need from me right now, for this task, to move forward?*

> **"** *Your leadership style isn't a preference or a personality; it's your influence strategy.*

This connects directly back to chapter 1, where we defined leadership as influence—the ability to shape outcomes, behaviors, and results through your actions. Step Three is simply the practical expression of that truth. Once you understand a performer's readiness, your job is to select the influence behavior that matches the moment. With the right match, influence becomes a catalyst for growth. And that sets the stage for what comes next: learning how to manage the movement as readiness rises, dips, and evolves over time.

Chapter 7 Review

Here are the key takeaways from chapter 7:

- Step Three (Match and Communicate Leader Response) is about adapting your leadership style to the performer's readiness for the task.
- Flexibility means you can use all four styles; adaptability means you choose the right style at the right time.
- The four styles align with readiness levels

    - **S1: Directing**—High task / low relationship
    - **S2: Coaching**—High task / high relationship
    - **S3: Supporting**—Low task / high relationship
    - **S4: Delegating**—Low task / low relationship

- No style is "best"—the best style is the one that matches the performer's ability and willingness for the task.
- Each style depends on intentional communication; when readiness is misdiagnosed, even well-meant communication can miss the mark.
- Common mismatches result in overleading or underleading and create frustration, stalled growth, and declining confidence.
- Self-awareness and openness to feedback help leaders strengthen their range and adapt with intention.

Nothing Stays the Same

Step Four: Manage the Movement

A week into the app project, Hana can tell Michael's making steady progress. He's providing strong updates, and the work is moving in the right direction. But then she starts getting an increasing number of messages from Michael where he's double-, and even triple-checking decisions they've made. He seems to be questioning himself.

For Hana, that's actually a positive sign. She's seen this same thing happen with other developers. Sometimes, when they're putting a new plan into motion, their skill level is actually growing but on full display, and they get nervous.

So Hana responds to Michael's message with an intentional mix of encouragement and empowerment: "You're headed in the right direction. The way you bridged the new scenario was spot-on. How do you think you'll handle the next one?"

His responses come back quicker, with more certainty, more like the Michael she knows.

In the next team meeting, he gives her a half smile before presenting his updates. When the feedback starts coming, he's quiet, and Hana can tell he's implementing her feedback from the one-on-one. He listens. He takes notes. He doesn't jump in to defend or explain. He's a bit stiff, and given how long Hana's worked with him, she knows it's taking everything in him to stay silent—but he does it!

Afterward, she pulls him aside. "Nice work in there. Let's debrief how that felt in our next one-on-one."

During that conversation Michael admits the silence was uncomfortable, but he also realized something: Not every idea is something he needs to act on. Some people just want to be heard. Some insights are genuinely helpful. Hana's proud of Michael's obvious growth.

Then two weeks before launch, things get rough. The usual VP of sales is out, and the director fills in at their weekly meeting. Mid-discussion, he tosses out brand-new UX ideas, and Michael about loses it. The project is two weeks from release—what is he supposed to do with this?

Before he can respond, Hana jumps in. "Great ideas," she says calmly. "Let's capture them for a future update."

Michael leaves the meeting feeling grateful for Hana but also discouraged. "I thought I was past this," he says when she catches up with him.

"You're fine," Hana says. "This is normal. Let's walk."

This is a brief glimpse into what a person's development journey truly looks like, with moments of progress, then hesitation, another step forward, and then an occasional slip back. But leaders, like Hana, move with their people. They adapt their approach. They notice the signs of progression and regression, and they stay steady when confidence soars, supportive when certainty dips, and clear when frustration spikes. The role of the leader is never done.

Readiness Is Always Moving

It's unrealistic to expect every follower to reach R4 for every task on a smooth path with limited turbulence. And that's not even really the leader's goal. The goal is to give people the right amount of support and direction they need *right now*. As you saw with Hana and Michael, someone can make amazing progress one week and then hit hesitation or new challenges the next. Even when someone approaches R4, something about the work will inevitably change; there'll be new priorities, shifting contexts, and fresh nuances, and the process begins again.

In other words Performance Readiness® is never fixed. People and performance are always moving. Circumstances change. Motivation fluctuates. Confidence rises and falls. A leader's job is to notice those shifts and respond accordingly.

> " *Performance Readiness® is never fixed. People and performance are always moving.*

The Situational Leadership® Model sits atop decades of research and is designed to accelerate development by giving people what they need when they need it. Leaders strengthen both ability and confidence by aligning their style with readiness, taking responsibility for training, mentoring, and supporting continued growth.

Performance Readiness®

HIGH	MODERATE		LOW
R4	**R3**	**R2**	**R1**
Able and Confident and Willing	**Able but Insecure or Unwilling**	**Unable but Confident or Willing**	**Unable and Insecure or Unwilling**
Self Directed		**Leader Directed**	

The bell curve in the model reflects this dynamic movement. Leadership behaviors should transition smoothly from one style to the next, as readiness increases or decreases. As someone advances from R1 to R2, leaders gradually reduce task direction and increase supportive behavior. As they progress from R3 to R4, leaders slowly release control, dialing back both task and relationship behaviors as the performer approaches autonomy. And when confidence dips or conditions shift, readiness can regress, requiring leaders to lean back in with more support. You move along the curve in both directions, meeting people exactly where they are.

> " *When change hits, readiness shifts.*

People grow, plateau, and sometimes regress. Managing the Movement—the fourth step in the model—is all about recognizing those shifts and responding effectively to create (and *recreate*) positive momentum. This involves circling back to Step Two (and when expectations or conditions change, back to Step One) over and over again, continually assessing readiness as circumstances, motivation, and confidence change. This is the skill of advancing: intentionally guiding progress, sustaining motivation, and keeping development in motion.

When Performance Readiness® increases, that's development—gaining the ability and confidence needed for greater autonomy. When it decreases, that's regression—a dip in motivation, confidence, or demonstrated skill for a once-familiar task. Effective leaders stay aware of these shifts and lead accordingly.

The Development Cycle

Development represents the growth and incremental improvement a person demonstrates for a specific task. On the Performance Readiness® continuum, ability increases from low to high as the individual progresses from R1 to R4.

When someone moves from R1 to R2, that progress takes place on the right side of the model. At this point the leader remains highly involved, making decisions about the task, initiating discussions, and checking for understanding and alignment. And on this side of the model, confidence has a lot to do with the involvement of the leader.

Situational Leadership®
Influence Behaviors

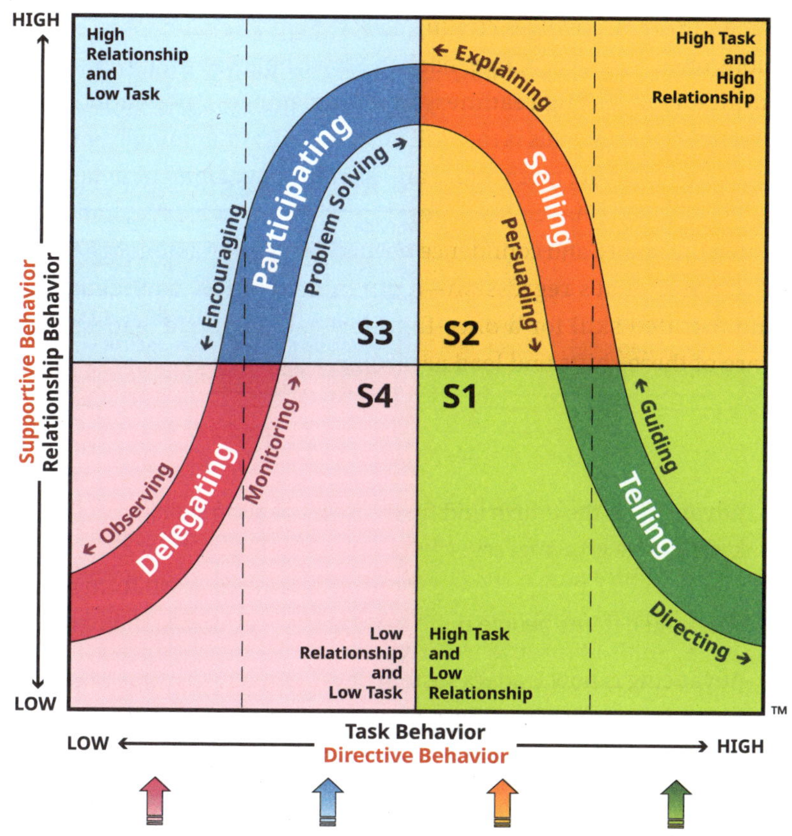

Performance Readiness®

	HIGH	MODERATE		LOW
	R4	R3	R2	R1
	Able and Confident and Willing	Able but Insecure or Unwilling	Unable but Confident or Willing	Unable and Insecure or Unwilling

Self Directed | Leader Directed

As the individual begins transitioning to the left side of the model, toward self-direction, something interesting happens: *Confidence often dips.* Between R2 and R3, as the leader steps back to allow more owner-ship, the performer's confidence must begin to come from within rather than from external validation. You saw this with Michael—his skill was rising, but his confidence wavered as Hana gave him more space.

Performance Readiness®

HIGH	MODERATE		LOW
R4	**R3**	**R2**	**R1**
Able and Confident and Willing ← →	Able but Insecure or Unwilling	Unable but Confident or Willing ← →	Unable and Insecure or Unwilling

Self Directed   **Leader Directed**

As Performance Readiness® moves along the continuum, leader behavior shifts too. There are practical steps leaders can take to accel-erate both ability and willingness. The words surrounding the curve of the Situational Leadership® Model capture this progression.

In S1, guiding bridges to S2, where the focus becomes selling—building understanding and buy-in. As the individual nears S3, the leader moves into more explaining, helping connect the dots between competence and confidence. On the left side of the model, task direction decreases while relationship support increases. The leader provides more encouraging behaviors to strengthen willingness and address wavering confidence.

As the individual develops mastery and autonomy in R4, the leader shifts into observing and delegating, remaining available but no longer directing. By the way delegating doesn't mean walking away; it means staying accessible, checking in, and ensuring continued success.

Although we've described the continuum in a linear way, de-velopment rarely follows a straight path. Someone might begin at R2 for a task, skipping R1 entirely. Others may move from R1 to R4 in a single jump, especially when the task is simple or familiar. This is why revisiting Step Two regularly is essential. You can't assume a performer will develop exactly as you expect. When leaders make that assumption, mismatches follow, and development stalls.

To maximize development efforts, leaders can rely on a set of proven practices that strengthen awareness and adaptability. These include the following:

- **Leading with intention**: Staying deliberate about your approach and paying close attention to its impact
- **Developing awareness**: Observing readiness cues and noticing shifts in ability and motivation
- **Focusing on alignment**: Ensuring clarity around goals, roles, and expectations
- **Asking questions**: Inviting reflection and ownership rather than simply giving direction
- **Empathizing with others**: Understanding what might be affecting willingness or confidence
- **Building trust**: Creating psychological safety so people can stretch and grow
- **Remaining flexible**: Adjusting your style as readiness changes

As you apply these practices, take time to reflect on where you have the greatest opportunity to grow your own leadership. Consider which of these areas you naturally excel in and which might benefit from greater focus. Development, after all, doesn't stop with your team; it continues with you.

Advancing Activities

Leaders grow, and help others grow, in so many ways. Some of the most impactful include the following:

- Observing work and providing meaningful feedback
- Setting clear priorities
- Coaching for skill and confidence

- Supporting people through challenges and helping them refocus
- Enabling growth by developing new skills
- Guiding career planning and progression
- Modeling a culture of continuous learning
- Creating an environment where people can perform at their best

Through the Lens of Regression

Up to this point, we've explored the Situational Leadership® process primarily through the lens of development. Now let's look at it through the lens of regression. The good news is that the leadership process doesn't change; the same steps still apply.

When an individual's performance for a task starts to slip, it's usually because something in their situation has changed. Responsibilities may have expanded, expectations may have shifted, or external pressures may be weighing them down. Sometimes regression has nothing to do with skill at all. A high-performing team member can suddenly miss deadlines simply because they're navigating intense personal stress, such as lack of sleep, housing instability, or family pressures. Their ability hasn't changed, but their confidence, energy, and focus have. The shift in situation causes the regression.

Whatever the cause, the first move for a Situational Leader is to revisit Step One to understand and align on what's different now. *What's changed about the task? How have expectations evolved?* By acknowledging these shifts and realigning on the specific task, the leader and individual can get back on the same page.

From there, Step Two involves reassessing Performance Readiness®. The leader evaluates the individual's current ability and their willingness for the task. This assessment should reflect the performer's current state, not where they were before the regression occurred. The best leaders engage the individual in this conversation to uncover what's driving the change and confirm alignment on their present readiness. In Step Three the leader adapts their approach to meet the individual's current performance needs.

The most common regression pattern occurs from R4 to R3, where the performer still has the skill to succeed but has lost motivation, confidence, or commitment. In this case a high-relationship, low-task approach has the greatest chance of success. That means spending more time connecting, listening, and rebuilding confidence rather than overdirecting the work.

The key with managing regression is to recognize the signs early and intervene quickly. Each regression scenario presents its own challenge, whether it's recognizing when the task has changed, understanding how expectations have shifted, identifying the root cause, or adjusting your leadership style to match current needs. The Situational Leadership® Model equips you to address all of them with awareness, agility, and intentional communication that restores both confidence and performance.

Humans Are Nuanced—Your Leadership Should Be Too

The Situational Leadership® Model is a probability model. It guides you to the most likely correct leadership style for a given situation, but that doesn't mean we remove nuance from our approach.

The overall direction in this step is simple: Match your leadership style to the performer's current Performance Readiness® Level. But regression is rarely simple. People are complex. Situations are complex. Often the best first move before applying a style in a regression scenario is to pause and have a conversation.

Consider not only what the performer needs to succeed at the task but also what they need *as a person*. Coming in too strong—with heavy, directive instruction for someone who has slipped from R4 to R1—can feel more like a reprimand than support.

Just because you're reassessing someone's current Performance Readiness® doesn't mean you ignore the context of their past performance. Acknowledging the full situation and working together to create a plan to get their performance back on track can be both grounding and motivating for the follower.

The Scale of Change

When an individual's performance begins to slip, it's rarely random. Regression usually stems from change. In other words something about the person, their role, or their environment has shifted. Change is constant, and it affects everyone in some way every day. When it happens, a person's Performance Readiness® often shifts with it because the knowledge, experience, or skill that once applied may no longer fit the new reality. Those shifts can influence confidence, commitment, and motivation, sometimes subtly, sometimes dramatically.

Situational Leaders "manage the movement" by staying attuned to these changes and understanding how they affect readiness. Change can be welcome or unwelcome, predictable or unexpected, but it always affects performance. To better understand this, we can look at three levels of change that most people experience: personal, professional, and organizational.

Personal Change

Personal change is the most individual and often the least visible to others. These are the events and transitions that deeply influence a person's mindset, energy, and emotional bandwidth, sometimes in ways that never surface in the workplace.

A personal change could be positive, such as training for a marathon, welcoming a new family member, or buying a home. It could also be challenging, such as managing an illness, caring for an aging parent, or navigating a major life loss.

Even positive changes can disrupt performance. A new goal or responsibility outside work might redirect focus or energy. Meanwhile, difficult personal changes can deplete confidence, commitment, and motivation. Every individual reacts differently, which is why leaders need to stay observant, curious, and empathetic. Awareness of life's smaller shifts often helps leaders support their people before minor disruptions turn into larger regressions.

Professional Change

Professional change occurs within the work itself, when tasks, expectations, or circumstances around a role evolve. Some of these changes are obvious: a promotion, a new project, or a shift to remote work. Others are more subtle but equally impactful: new tools or processes, a change in team composition, or a different reporting structure.

Consider the widespread move to virtual work environments. For many, that change altered everything about how people communicated, collaborated, and measured success. Ability and willingness both shifted because the rules of the task changed.

Professional change can also cut both ways. Being passed over for a promotion might diminish confidence or motivation, while receiving an award for performance can strengthen both. The key for leaders is to notice the shift and rediagnose readiness accordingly rather than assuming someone's performance will automatically remain steady or keep improving.

Organizational Change

At the broadest level, organizational change affects entire teams or companies. These are the transformations that ripple through structures, systems, and strategies: reorganizations, mergers, leadership changes, new business models, or shifts in mission and priorities.

For example, a reorganization could mean new reporting lines, new leaders, or new expectations. A change in product or service offerings could demand new skills or technical knowledge. Even a seemingly positive shift, such as rapid growth, can create stress and uncertainty as people adjust to new demands.

Not everyone will experience organizational change in the same way. What feels like an exciting opportunity for one person can feel overwhelming for another. Effective leaders understand these differences and stay close enough to notice how their people are responding.

Change is inevitable, and with it comes fluctuation in ability and willingness. What separates great leaders from the rest is their ability to recognize those moments quickly, rediagnose readiness, and adjust their leadership style to meet their people where they are to help them move forward again. We'll explore how to lead through change in more depth in chapter 10, but for now that awareness starts with recognizing the cues that signal a shift in readiness.

Recognizing and Responding to Regression

Regression can look different for everyone. It may show up as subtle shifts in attitude or energy or as clear drops in performance or engagement. A typically cooperative person might become inflexible. Someone who's usually proactive might begin waiting for direction. Small shifts like these often reveal that something deeper has changed. Continually observing performance trends and staying alert to these behavioral cues allows leaders to intervene early.

Signs of Regression

Here are some examples of changes that could indicate regression:

- Someone is usually cooperative but has become inflexible.
- Someone composed becomes agitated.
- Someone self-assured becomes fearful.
- Someone reliable becomes inconsistent.
- Someone punctual becomes tardy.
- Someone prepared becomes unprepared.
- Someone producing withholds performance.

- Someone receptive becomes defensive.
- Someone decisive becomes cautious.
- Someone attentive becomes forgetful.
- Someone enthusiastic becomes apathetic.
- Someone accessible becomes unavailable.
- Someone proactive starts to avoid.

In many cases short-term performance slippage is much more about willingness than ability. It's not that someone's skill has disappeared; it's that their motivation, confidence, or commitment has wavered. In Situational Leadership® terms, when regression happens, movement on the Performance Readiness® continuum travels from left to right—away from autonomy and toward the need for more structure and support.

It's important to remember that regression isn't linear. People don't move neatly from one level to the next on the way down. For example, someone in R3 (able but unwilling) isn't going to pass through R2 (unable but willing and confident). Instead, regression tends to show up in a few common (but *nonsequential*) patterns. Here are three we see most often:

R2 → R1: The Enthusiastic Beginner Who Loses Heart

Unable but Confident or Willing (R2)
Unable and Insecure or Unwilling (R1)

This can happen when the excitement that comes with a new task isn't met with the kind of support the performer needs. They start wondering, *Does anybody around here care?* Another version shows up in premature delegation (S4 → R2). Someone takes on more than they're ready for, struggles, gets embarrassed, and slides back to R1: "I'm never volunteering for anything else around here again."

R4 → R3: The Thrill Is Gone

Able and Confident and Willing (R4)
Able but Insecure or Unwilling (R3)

This is one of the most common. Once a performer masters a task, the novelty can fade, and without fresh challenges or meaningful connection, motivation dips, even though the person's skill remains high.

R3 → R1: The Confidence Collapse

Able but Insecure or Unwilling (R3)
Unable and Insecure or Unwilling (R1)

Sometimes a highly capable performer takes a hard hit to willingness or confidence because of outside pressures such as a missed promotion, personal stress, conflict, or discouragement. They might consciously disengage or simply lose the motivation to apply the skills they already have. They may still be capable of performing, but if they're not currently doing so at a sustained, acceptable level, they're unable.

These patterns remind leaders that a drop in performance rarely initiates with a drop in ability. More often, something in the situation or the follower's willingness has shifted, and the leader needs to shift with it.

Regaining Trust

When someone slides from R3 all the way back to R1, it's rarely about the task alone. Sometimes this kind of regression is rooted in their leader's actions—or inaction. And with it comes a loss of trust. Repairing that trust is essential before development can resume. Here's how to move forward:

- **Acknowledge your mistake:** Make sure the performer knows that you understand you let them down. Let them know how you'll avoid this in the future.

- **Establish clear next steps:** It's important that the follower knows you're not giving up on them. Communicate your expectations for yourself and the follower to get back on track. Depending on the circumstances around the regression, you might involve the follower in this process to gain buy-in.
- **Provide a matching leadership style:** The best thing you can do to build trust in your leadership is to provide a matching leadership style moving forward.

Ultimately, managing regression is about attention and adaptability. Leaders who stay connected to their people—watching, listening, and engaging with genuine care—are best equipped to recognize changes early and help others regain confidence, commitment, and momentum.

The Ongoing Work of Leadership

As we wrap up the four steps of leveraging the Situational Leadership® Model, you've probably noticed a consistent theme: The follower is at the center of it all. Returning to Step Two throughout Step Four is how you stay connected to what the follower needs right now. It's how you keep their readiness, their growth, and their success top of mind.

And as you may be realizing, the process doesn't truly end with Step Four. Managing the movement is the ongoing leadership you'll practice for as long as the task exists. That can feel like a lot at first, but with practice the entire process becomes second nature. You begin to see the movement. You start to anticipate the shifts. You get comfortable adjusting in real time.

In the next chapter, we'll zoom out and look at leadership from a broader perspective—how the ideas you've learned apply in the real world and help you navigate the challenges of the modern workplace. The Situational Leadership® Model and its four-step process equip you to use the approach. Now we'll explore the depth and context that turn an effective leader into a Situational Leader.

The Four Core Skills of Situational Leadership®

The Situational Leadership® process builds leaders who can turn potential into performance. Its four steps are supported by four timeless leadership skills that serve as the foundation for success.

- **Diagnose:** Understand the situation by assessing the task and the individual's level of Performance Readiness®.
- **Adapt:** Choose the leadership approach that best aligns with the individual's current performance needs.
- **Communicate:** Deliver your chosen style clearly and effectively to ensure understanding and buy-in.
- **Advance:** Act as a catalyst for progress by accelerating development or redirecting regression.

Mastering these four skills enables leaders to stay flexible, intentional, and connected, helping people grow and keeping performance moving forward.

Chapter 8 Review

Here are the key takeaways from chapter 8:

- Step Four (Manage the Movement) requires leaders to revisit Step Two regularly and reassess what the performer needs right now.
- Performance Readiness® is rarely linear. Ability and willingness rise and fall as tasks, circumstances, and confidence shift.
- Performers can move between levels at any time. When readiness increases, that's development; when it decreases, that's regression.
- Effective leaders adjust their leadership style smoothly as readiness increases or decreases, offering the right balance of direction and support.
- Personal, professional, or organizational change is one of the most common drivers of regression.

- Managing movement means staying connected, noticing readiness cues early, and responding quickly to keep growth in motion.

Reflect and Apply

Before you move on, take a moment to reflect on how this chapter applies to your leadership today.

1. Where have you seen someone's confidence or motivation shift recently?
2. When was the last time you intentionally *re*diagnosed someone's readiness for a familiar task?
3. What leadership style adjustment might help someone regain momentum right now?

Managing Performance

At CLS, one of the most important things we do is study global work-force challenges. Every day we talk with senior executives, managers, individual contributors, our partners, and other training organizations about what's challenging right now and what's changing in their world of work. We listen to their stories, their struggles, and their successes.

The context is always shifting. Artificial intelligence. Remote and hybrid work. Evolving expectations of what leadership should look like. These forces can make today's challenges feel completely new. But after more than fifty-five years of studying leadership, we've learned that, while the landscape may change, the core challenges remain surprisingly consistent. Why? Because leadership has always been about shifting dynamics.

> *After more than fifty-five years of studying leadership, we've learned that, while the landscape may change, the core challenges remain surprisingly consistent. Why? Because leadership has always been about shifting dynamics.*

These global shifts don't just affect strategy and structure; they influence how people show up at work. They shape motivation, communication, and trust. And as a leader, they shape how you show up too. Even though the Situational Leadership® Model focuses on the task and the follower, leadership never happens in isolation. Every interaction is influenced by the broader environment in which people live and work, an important reminder of the leadership equation you encountered in the introduction.

Even though the Situational Leadership® Model focuses on the task and follower, a great leader still pays attention to the larger variables at play. The better you understand what's happening around your people—the pressures, priorities, and possibilities that define their experience—the more effectively you can lead them. And there's no better way to navigate those human dynamics than by applying this model.

Need to navigate the demands of the modern workplace? The world of work today requires more than efficiency; it requires *empathy*. (See, it always comes back to that balance between success and engagement.) Employees want flexibility and stability, but they also want connection and purpose. The Situational Leadership® framework helps leaders build trust, foster respect, and create environments where people feel safe enough to take risks, think creatively, and grow. It gives you a process for identifying talent, clarifying expectations, and inspiring people to pursue a shared vision.

Need to develop leaders at every level? Leadership is no longer tied to a title; it's a skill. Organizations that intentionally grow leadership competencies across every layer of the business create cultures of accountability, collaboration, and resilience. The Situational Leadership® Model provides a shared language for influence that helps everyone lead—up, down, and across the organization.

In fact, the top five global workforce challenges we've identified, which continue to shape how organizations operate today, can all be addressed through the Situational Leadership® Model.

- **Modern Workplace Leadership:** Building trust, flexibility, and belonging in evolving environments
- **Leadership as a Skill**: Developing leadership capabilities at every level
- **Performance Leadership:** Turning potential into results through clarity, coaching, and accountability

- **Skilling Talent:** Preparing people with the competence and confidence to meet the demands of tomorrow
- **Change Leadership:** Guiding people through uncertainty with empathy, communication, and courage

Of all these challenges, performance leadership sits at the center. Because every other challenge—adapting to the modern workplace, growing new leaders, building skills, or navigating change—depends on people's ability to perform at their best. The future of work will always depend on how well leaders can turn potential into results—consistently, sustainably, and rapidly. That's where the Situational Leadership® Model proves its lasting power.

> **"** *The future of work will always depend on how well leaders can turn potential into results—consistently, sustainably, and rapidly.*

With this model as your foundation, you can give people what they need to grow and perform at their best. In the paragraphs that follow, we'll explore how the model equips you to manage performance in real time, on a larger scale, to create the conditions where high performance can thrive.

Turning Potential into Performance

Every organization is full of potential, people with knowledge, ambition, and the desire to contribute at a higher level. But potential alone doesn't move the needle. The difference between potential and performance is—you guessed it!—leadership.

Leaders who can translate potential into results are the ones who meet today's challenges head-on. These leaders aren't just developing people; they're accelerating growth, shortening the gap between learning and mastery. That's what we call time to autonomy: the period it takes for someone to move from novice (R1) to expert (R4), from needing direction to operating independently.

Time to autonomy looks different for everyone. It depends on the individual, their experience, and the complexity of the task. But one thing remains constant: An adaptive leader can shorten that journey. By diagnosing readiness, matching leadership style, and adjusting as development unfolds, leaders help people gain competence and confidence faster. Which means they can perform at higher levels sooner.

Think about the cost of onboarding a new employee. Many organizations follow thirty-, sixty-, or ninety-day plans, yet onboarding often stretches far beyond those timelines. Skilled employees spend months training others, diverting time and resources from their own work. Now imagine cutting that ramp-up time in half by applying the Situational Leadership® process to every new task. That's exactly what the model was designed to do!

One of our local clients, an HVAC company, experienced this first-hand. Their most senior, five-star technicians were being lured away by competitors. (However, retention wasn't the issue we were trying to solve here.) When those technicians left, the company filled the roles with new hires, but few of them were rated above two stars. The only remaining five-star technician was stretched thin trying to teach others how to solve the most complex problems. As a result, response times slowed dramatically, and customers started leaving.

The company quickly realized that their time to autonomy (the three to five years it took to train a technician to five stars) was now driving every other business outcome. Here's where the Situational Leadership® Model made a difference. Supervisors were trained in the framework, and they learned how to use it to accelerate development. As they applied the model consistently, they not only developed new technicians faster; they also helped stabilize the team and reduce further loss of top talent. Talk about a win-win!

Each technician represented more than a million dollars of bottom-line value in training time. Even shaving a few months off that development timeline created meaningful savings and protected customer relationships. And because the model boosted both development and day-to-day support, it also helped keep their experienced R4 technicians around while they built up the next generation.

The same principle applies everywhere. How good are you at keeping your top performers? How effectively are you developing the talent you already have? How many additional features could your software team release if they became more efficient? How much more revenue could a salesperson generate if she reached R4 in the critical tasks of her job sooner? Your ability to break roles into tasks and then help people advance through mastery of those tasks is what translates leadership into real organizational impact.

Reducing time to autonomy is one of the most valuable contributions a leader can make. Not only does it improve morale and efficiency, but it drives measurable results. Faster development means greater productivity, stronger performance, and real financial impact.

Performance Conversations

In most organizations the word "performance" immediately signals something negative—an issue, a correction, a formal evaluation. But in the Situational Leadership® Model, every conversation about work is a performance conversation. Performance Readiness® isn't good or bad; it simply describes what someone needs right now to succeed at a task. And because readiness is always changing, conversations about performance should be happening all the time.

That's why the model belongs in everyday leadership—as the language you use to set objectives, give feedback, and keep work moving. Most performance management systems begin with objectives, end with evaluation, and rely on feedback in between. Situational Leadership® supports all three. You establish objectives differently with an R1 for a task than you do with someone at R4. You give feedback differently to someone who's unsure than to someone who's confident and performing. And you adjust your leadership approach as readiness shifts.

So instead of saving "performance conversations" for formal reviews, you bring them into the daily rhythm of your team. Every one-on-one, every team meeting, every check-in is an opportunity to apply the model. It's easy to slip into autopilot during routine discussions, but those everyday moments define the culture of your work environment more than anything else.

In each interaction ask yourself the following:

- Are we aligned on the task?
- Are we aligned on current performance?
- Am I meeting this person's needs with the right balance of task and relationship behavior?

Those questions guide your conversations and show you where more dialogue or coaching is needed.

When performance conversations happen every day, and feedback is frequent, natural, and connected to the work happening right now, people develop quicker. The conversations feel lighter, more constructive, and far less stressful. Over time your team grows more comfortable talking about what they need for success, and many will even start initiating those conversations themselves.

When motivation is high and progress is steady, friction decreases. Small issues get addressed early and don't have the chance to become something bigger. And when a larger intervention is needed, it's not a surprise; it's simply the next step in an ongoing dialogue built on trust and mutual accountability.

Creating Relationships Around the Work

One of the most effective ways to foster honest, productive performance conversations is to build strong relationships around the work. We're talking about referent power here—the kind of influence that comes from genuine connection.

Remember, referent power is earned slowly, over countless interactions. It's built when people feel seen, valued, and heard. When you take the time to listen well, respond thoughtfully, and lead with people (rather than *over* them), you create a feedback loop of respect. They listen because you listen. They engage because you engage.

When someone cares about the relationship, they don't want to let you down. They're more open to feedback, more eager to learn, and more committed to shared success. That's why building strong, healthy leader–follower relationships is a core driver of performance.

When people feel supported and challenged in equal measure, engagement rises, and ability improves even faster.

Leading Performance into the Future

The future of work will keep changing with new tools, new expectations, and new challenges. But one thing remains constant: Leadership is still measured by performance. Luckily, Situational Leadership® is also a language of performance leadership. It gives leaders a practical way to strengthen engagement, improve results, and retain their best people.

Over time the Situational Leadership® approach builds autonomy. As people grow, leaders shift from directing to coaching to supporting to delegating, always matching what the work requires. You're not just managing tasks—you're developing performers. And as individuals gain confidence and competence, teams become more resilient and more self-reliant.

> **"** *You're not just managing tasks—
> you're developing performers.*

It also makes accountability personal and achievable. When performance conversations happen daily, not just quarterly, accountability becomes a shared commitment. Leader and follower take ownership together. Expectations stay clear. Misalignment surfaces early. And contribution becomes something people step toward, not something they fear.

And because the model is task-specific and behavior-based, it introduces and reinforces that common language of performance. That consistency strengthens communication between leaders and followers, across functions, and throughout the organization.

All this leads to what every organization depends on:

Success
Delivering meaningful results

Engagement
Creating an environment where people feel energized, challenged, and supported

Retention
Keeping your best people growing and choosing to stay

Everything in this chapter—accelerating development, shortening time to autonomy, holding frequent performance conversations, building trust—directly strengthens those outcomes. Success improves because expectations are clear. Engagement rises because people feel seen and supported. Retention grows because great leaders build relationships worth staying for.

But sustaining performance doesn't happen in a static environment. The context around your people will keep shifting, and your role in this dynamic environment isn't just to manage performance; it's to help people maintain it through change. That's where we turn next. Because even the highest-performing teams will struggle if they can't navigate disruption together.

The Situational Leadership® Model gives you the framework to do both: to sustain performance today and to lead people confidently into tomorrow. It helps you meet people where they are, guide them where they need to go, and build the trust that keeps performance steady through uncertainty.

Why Situational Leadership® Drives Performance

1. Aligns behavior with performance needs

Situational Leadership® helps leaders match the right mix of direction and support to a person's ability and willingness on a specific task.

2. Closes the gap between potential and results

Even capable people underperform when they're unclear or unsupported. The model helps leaders diagnose what's missing and address it in real time.

3. Builds autonomy over time

By moving from directing → coaching → supporting → delegating as readiness grows, leaders not only manage performance; they develop performers.

4. Makes accountability shared and achievable

Frequent conversations create mutual ownership of goals, expectations, and outcomes.

5. Creates a common language

Because it's task-specific and behavior-based, Situational Leadership® gives teams and organizations a consistent, repeatable way to talk about performance.

Chapter 9 Review

Here are the key takeaways from chapter 9:

- The top five global workplace challenges are Modern Workplace Leadership, Leadership as a Skill, Performance Leadership, Skilling Talent, and Change Leadership.

- The Situational Leadership® Model equips leaders to navigate all these challenges by aligning direction and support with what people need *right now.*
- Of the five global workforce challenges, performance leadership sits at the center, because every other challenge depends on people's ability to perform.
- Time to autonomy (or the journey from R1 to R4) can be shortened when leaders diagnose accurately and match their style intentionally.
- Daily performance conversations are more important than formal reviews; readiness changes constantly, so alignment must be ongoing.
- Strong performance depends on clarity, trust, and consistent dialogue. Leaders who build relationships around the work accelerate development and strengthen engagement.
- The Situational Leadership® Model closes the gap between potential and results by providing a practical, repeatable way to develop performers and sustain accountability.

Reflect and Apply

Before you move on, take a moment to reflect on how this chapter applies to your leadership today.

1. Which global workforce challenge is most prevalent at your organization today?
2. Where could shortening time to autonomy have the biggest impact on your team?
3. How often are you having quick, task-focused performance conversations (not just formal reviews)?

Navigating Change

"The only constant in life is change."

"Change is inevitable."

"Buckle up—more change is coming!"

Are you rolling your eyes yet? We've heard these lines so often they barely register anymore. Years ago every new shift felt so dramatic. Now most of us think, *I'll deal with that change when it hits me in the face.* Intellectually, we understand that change is constant. But practically, we ignore it until we can't.

And honestly, it's no wonder. The pace really *has* accelerated. Accenture reports that the level of change affecting organizations has jumped 183 percent in recent years[6]—*183 percent!* Does that hit you hard? Does it surprise you? Probably not. Change has become the crowded subway we squeeze into every day—so normal we hardly notice the people packed in around us.

But leaders can't afford to ignore it. That acceleration has consequences. Gartner reports that employees' willingness to support enterprise change has dropped from 74 percent to 38 percent in less than a decade.[7] Yikes! Burnout is rising. Trust is eroding. Transformation fatigue is real.

And yet most organizations still struggle to manage change effectively. According to McKinsey, only one in three transformation initiatives actually succeeds.[8] In other words we're facing more change than ever while somehow becoming less equipped to navigate it. What's going on?

The problem is, we tend to treat change like a strategic or operational issue when, in reality, it's all about people. Yes, the systems are shifting. But who's responsible for those systems? Who feels the impact of every new process, decision, or disruption? Real people do. Change affects how they work, how they think, and how they feel. And in that disruption, people need something very specific: a steady, present, trustworthy leader. Someone who can help them regain a sense of control, move from uncertainty to action, and lead with both empathy and clarity at the same time.

Leadership directly influences performance, and performance often determines whether change succeeds or fails. When leaders get lost or overwhelmed, teams crumble. But when leaders stay present, empathetic, and decisive, people find the courage to move forward. That's where the Situational Leadership® Model shines: It's a model for leading people through change.

The Change Action Plan for Leaders

When facing significant change, consider these key actions:

- **Start with the facts:** Acknowledge the emotions that surface, but return to what's true. What's the situation? What needs to happen next?
- **Make hard decisions:** Evaluate your options and act on facts, not feelings.
- **Create a positive vision:** Picture success two years from now. What will your team and organization look like once you've navigated this change well? Paint a clear, hopeful picture of that future.
- **Take action:** Communicate the vision, lead with confidence, and do what needs to be done.

Leading Change Through the Four Steps

The Situational Leadership® Model is built on a Theory Y view of people, the belief that individuals want to contribute, are capable of growth, and can rise to meet new expectations when they're supported in the right way. When you adjust your approach to meet someone's needs in the moment, you accelerate their learning and help them build mastery.

That's true at the individual level, and it's just as true at the organizational level. The same four-step process that helps you develop a performer can help you guide an entire team through uncertainty or transformation.

Here's what that looks like when everything around you is shifting:

Step 1: Identify the Specific Task (Bring the Change into Focus)

Think back to the forest–tree–leaf analogy from chapter 5. Consider your change initiative as the "forest"—the big picture. For example, imagine an organizational merger. That's the forest.

Within that, you and your team should align on the major components of the change—the "trees"—such as two sales departments coming together under the parent brand.

From there, break the change down into the "leaves," or the specific tasks each person must complete, such as the newly combined sales team learning an expanded product line. Most of these tasks will be new for both you and your followers, so take the time to ensure everyone's on the same page.

Step 2: Assess Current Performance Readiness® (See What Change Is Asking of People)

Once you've identified the tasks that make up the change, the next step is understanding what those tasks require from your team. That's where Performance Readiness® becomes essential. It helps you see not just what needs to get done but how prepared each person is to do it.

You can look at readiness on two levels. There's the big-picture level—your team's overall ability and motivation for the change initiative as a whole. And then there's the more individual level—how prepared they are for the specific responsibilities tied to their part of the change.

For any change-related task, you can start with the following two simple questions:

- Are they performing at a sustained, acceptable level? (Ability!)
- Are they confident, committed, and motivated? (Willingness!)

In most cases the answer to both is "not yet." Change brings something unfamiliar. Which means individuals will almost always start on the right side of the Situational Leadership® Model for change-related tasks because they haven't had the chance to demonstrate ability. Even strong performers can find themselves at an R1 or R2 level when everything shifts. This is simply the reality of doing new work in a new context.

Begin where they are. Look for what they need in this moment, not what they could do in the past. Your role in the early stages is to help them get oriented, rebuild clarity, and gain early wins so their readiness and confidence can grow with experience.

Step 3: Match and Communicate Leadership Response (Guide Their First Uncertain Steps)

Once you've assessed where people are starting—their personal ability and willingness, as well as their overall readiness for the change—the next step is responding in a way that fits what you've seen. Remember, in moments of change, most performers begin on the right side of the Situational Leadership® Model. They haven't yet demonstrated ability in this new context, and unfamiliar tasks naturally create a need for more clarity and support.

This is where those more directive leadership styles become especially important. Our LEAD Assessment data shows that today's leaders are generally less comfortable with the leader-driven styles (S1 and S2) than previous generations. Yet those styles are exactly what people need in the early stages of change. When change arises, teams look for direction, someone to steady the moment and help them take their first uncertain steps forward.

Here's what that looks like in practice:

S1 ("I talk. I decide.")

When no one's developed ability yet, they need clear direction. An S1 approach gives your team the structure required to begin. You're clarifying what needs to happen and when it needs to happen so no one is left guessing.

S2 ("We talk. I decide.")

As people start to understand what's changing, they naturally bring questions, ideas, and reactions. S2 creates room for that dialogue. You're still providing direction, but now you're explaining the why, sharing context, and helping people make sense of what's shifting while still making the final call to maintain clarity and momentum.

In seasons of change, leaders need to be willing to use these styles even if they don't naturally gravitate toward them. This is what empowers people to build ability. You're not just helping them adjust to the change; you're helping them perform within it.

Step 4: Manage the Movement
(Stay with People as Readiness Shifts)

When change hits, people's Performance Readiness® rises and falls as the situation evolves. Someone who felt confident last month may feel thrown off-balance today. Someone who resisted the change at first may start to see the value and lean in. Your role is to stay close enough to notice those shifts.

Check in frequently. Pay attention to people's tone, energy, questions, and body language. This is when referent power really comes into play. The more your team believes you see them, hear them, and care about their success, the more willing they'll be to keep moving with you through uncertainty.

We saw this play out in Joshua's story from chapter 1. During his organization's leadership crisis, his team was suddenly thrust into unfamiliar territory, and they were looking for a stabilizing force. Joshua didn't have all the answers (in fact, he was feeling off-kilter himself!), but the trust he had built long before the crisis kept his people centered and committed. He paired that referent power with clear S1 direction, followed by S2 dialogue, to help people make sense of what was happening. Because of that combination of trust and appropriate style, they were willing to stay and keep moving with him through the uncertainty.

Managing the movement means you're continually adjusting your style as readiness changes, dialing task behavior up or down, increasing or easing relationship support, and helping people move step-by-step toward renewed confidence and sustained performance. In seasons of change, that steady presence is often what people remember most. Not that you had all the answers but that you stayed with them while they found their footing.

Get Real with Change (Early!)

When change hits, people instinctively look to their leader for stability. They want to know what's real, what's next, and whether they can trust the ground beneath them. Those first moments are so significant. *How* you communicate—your tone, your presence, your steadiness—can either anchor people or unsettle them further.

You don't need to have all the answers. You simply need to approach everything with a combination of empathy and clarity. To acknowledge what people feel without losing sight of where you're headed together. And while there's no perfect script for these moments, there are ways to prepare yourself so you can communicate with calm, credibility, and care.

Before you speak to your team, pause long enough to ground yourself. Make sure you understand the facts of the situation: what's changing, why it matters, and what you're able to share. Talk with your own leader. Ask the questions you need to ask. Process your emotions so you can show up calm and centered. Change often brings tough reactions; anticipating them helps you stay present when they surface.

When you do communicate, speak as part of the organization,

not outside of it. Use "we," even if the decision wasn't yours. People need to know you're aligned and informed, not distancing yourself out of discomfort. And if there are details you genuinely can't share, say so directly. That honesty builds the credibility you'll need in the days ahead.

Above all, point people toward what comes next. Change throws everyone off-balance, and direction restores a sense of control. End your message with a clear next step or, at minimum, the priorities you'll be focusing on together. If you can, reconnect the change to the larger vision or purpose your team cares about.

But communication certainly doesn't end with the announcement. In many ways it begins there. Change shakes people's sense of safety. Questions surface. Emotions rise. Some people get quiet. Others get loud. Each reaction is shaped by past experiences, personal fears, and private hopes. Staying fully present is really important at this stage. Make time for one-on-one conversations and adapt to the unique reactions and needs of each of your team members. Listen more than you speak. Show curiosity about what someone is feeling and why. When people feel seen, their anxiety eases; when they feel dismissed, it grows.

Communicating Through Change

In moments of change, people take their cues from you. These essentials help you communicate with steadiness:

1. **Prepare yourself.**
   Get clear on the facts, align with your leader, and settle your own emotions so you can show up grounded.

2. **Lead with empathy and clarity.**
   Acknowledge what people feel; say what you can, and be honest about what you can't.

3. **Point to what's next.**
   End with direction, immediate priorities, or the next step forward.

4. **Stay present.**
    Make space for conversations. Listen with curiosity and expect a range of reactions.

5. **Bring it back to the concrete.**
    Share a simple plan, explain the why, and begin with one achievable step to rebuild confidence.

Once emotions begin to settle, help your team refocus on what they can influence. This is where legitimate power, used with integrity, enables you to advance. Be transparent about the decisions being made and the reasons behind them. Share a simple, concrete plan that outlines goals, responsibilities, milestones, and the resources available.

And resist the temptation to solve everything at once. Big moves can overwhelm a team that's already stretched thin. Start with one achievable step, something small but meaningful, because quick wins rebuild confidence. They remind people they can make progress even when the horizon feels uncertain. And once confidence begins to return, momentum will follow. Change may unsettle and stretch people, but the way you diagnose, adapt, communicate, and advance through it can rebuild stability just as quickly.

Find Your Own Support

Leaders need support too. You can't lean on your team for emotional processing, but you can and should seek guidance elsewhere.

Talk with your supervisor, a mentor, an executive coach, or a trusted peer. Find a space where you can think aloud, process emotions, and regain perspective.

Leading through change is hard. Having your own support system helps you lead others from a place of steadiness and strength.

Creating a Culture of Change Ownership

During a recent coaching engagement, a director described her team as "strong individually but wobbly in the handoffs." Nothing was wrong with their skill; the struggle showed up in the gaps. Updates weren't consistent. Assumptions filled in where conversations should have happened. When a major restructuring was announced, those small gaps quickly widened. Later she reflected, "If we'd built better habits before the change, the change wouldn't have thrown us so far off-balance."

That experience is common—and preventable. When a team already knows how to align, adapt, and communicate in calm waters, they're far better prepared to do the same when the storm hits. A strong culture of change ownership grows from six essential traits, each supported by everyday habits that strengthen resilience over time.

Open Communication

Encourage open, honest dialogue that keeps people aligned and informed. Confirm understanding by repeating back key takeaways. Maintain regular one-on-ones and team touch-points to support clarity and connection.

Flexibility

Build the habit of adapting quickly to what's needed in the moment. Leave a margin for unexpected needs. When challenges arise, identify several possible solutions before choosing one. Stay current by reviewing industry case studies and considering how your organization might respond in similar situations.

Curiosity

Approach change with questions and an open mind rather than fear or resistance. Set aside a few minutes each day to explore new ideas or industry innovations. Ask colleagues for their perspectives on shared challenges. Check in regularly about how roles, goals, or responsibilities may be evolving.

Creativity

Encourage fresh thinking and experimentation. Revisit routine tasks and try one small improvement each week. At the end of each week, reflect on what worked and consider how processes could be simplified or improved.

Accountability

Promote shared ownership of results and progress. Ask for clear success metrics for each task. Every few weeks review where you're progressing or regressing. Add a "challenges" section to your one-on-one notes to track where additional support may be needed.

Optimism

Keep your team focused on possibilities instead of problems. End each day by writing down one thing that strengthened confidence or motivation. Share something positive or encouraging with your team each week.

The most effective change initiatives are the ones where everyone—from the C-suite to the front line—plays an active role in moving the organization forward. That kind of alignment doesn't start when change begins. It's built earlier, in the steady seasons, when leaders consistently invest in teamwork, communication, and positivity.

The World Needs Your Leadership

Nothing can replace the heart and motivation a great leader brings. There's no situation you can't face, no challenge you can't overcome, when you begin with trust and lead with integrity.

Organizations have a choice. They can motivate through safety, policies, and perks, or they can invest in people. The first approach may work for a while, but when hard times come, there's nothing to draw on. Without trust, people disengage. They quit and leave, or far worse, they quit and stay!

> **"** *Organizations have a choice. They can motivate through safety, policies, and perks, or they can invest in people.*

Leaders who believe in people choose differently. They invest in development, in growth, in leadership itself. And what they get in return is powerful: institutional wisdom, adaptability, resilience, and a workforce that shows up with purpose.

Weathering change as a leader isn't easy. You'll spend long hours listening to fear, frustration, and fatigue. You'll reassure, recalibrate, and respond with empathy. You'll adjust your leadership style as your people regain readiness, helping them move from uncertainty to action. And when they're ready, you'll point them toward the future.

That's what great leaders do. They navigate change with finesse. They meet it head-on. Your leadership has the power to shape how others experience some of the hardest moments of their professional lives. It can steady people when everything around them feels unstable. It can transform disruption into growth. The world needs that kind of leadership—*your* leadership—now more than ever.

So when change comes again, as it always will, how will you lead?

Chapter 10 Review

Here are the key takeaways from chapter 10:

- Change is accelerating, and people's willingness to support it is declining.

- Organizations often treat change as a strategy problem when it's actually a people problem.
- During disruption, people need a steady, present, trustworthy leader who brings both empathy and clarity.
- The Situational Leadership® Model equips leaders to navigate change successfully by diagnosing what people need in the moment and adjusting accordingly.
- Most performers start on the right side of the Situational Leadership® Model during change because the work is new, even if they're highly capable.
- Early in change, teams need more S1 and S2 leadership—clear direction, structure, context, and reassurance.
- Communication is vital during change: Leaders need to ground themselves in facts, acknowledge emotions, be honest, and point to what comes next.
- Teams navigate change better when habits of openness, flexibility, curiosity, creativity, accountability, and optimism already exist.

Reflect and Apply

Before you move on, take a moment to reflect on how this chapter applies to your leadership today.

1. How openly does your team communicate right now?
2. What is your team's capacity for creativity?
3. What could you do to strengthen the optimism of your team about the future?

Conclusion

Throughout this book we've explored effective leadership. We've seen that leadership isn't a title or a position; it's influence. And influence depends on power—the potential we have to affect the behavior, attitudes, and performance of others.

We've discovered that how we lead is situational, because ultimately—*it depends*. People aren't simply "good" or "bad"; rather, their performance depends on the task and their experience and motivation to complete it. Additionally, their ability and willingness shifts from one assignment to the next, depending on a number of factors, including what's happening in their lives at that very moment.

We've learned to diagnose those shifts and better understand their impacts based on these two questions: *Are they?* and *Will they?* Those answers reveal what people need to succeed. These cues signal to leaders how they should respond with the right amount of direction and support. Sometimes that means stepping in and providing structure. Other times it means stepping back and empowering others to act.

The Situational Leadership® Model gives us a way to make sense of all the complexity. It teaches us to pause and diagnose before acting, to adapt our style to the readiness of the person in front of us, to communicate with clarity, and to advance performance by helping people move forward with both confidence and competence.

Ultimately, we've seen that effective leadership isn't about finding the perfect style; it's about developing the awareness and agility to choose the right response for the situation in front of us.

From Model to Mindset

Remember Margot?

These days you'd hardly recognize her. On Monday mornings her team still gathers for their sales meeting, but the energy in the room has changed. Margot starts with her newest rep, who's nervous about a big client call. "Let's walk through it together," she says, outlining what success looks like and modeling how to open the conversation. It's structured and clear and just what he needs to feel prepared.

Next, she turns to a rep who's been improving steadily but still second-guessing herself. "You've done this before," Margot reminds her. "What worked last time?" Together, they sketch a plan, with Margot coaching, encouraging, and helping her find her own rhythm.

Later that day she checks in with her top performer. Instead of giving direction, she simply asks, "What do you need from me to keep this moving?" He smiles. "Honestly? Just space." She laughs. "Done."

At home the same awareness shows up in smaller ways. When her daughter gets frustrated by a science project, Margot joins her at the table. "Show me where it's not working," she says, guiding her through one step and then backing off so her daughter can figure out the rest. That night, when her husband mentions a conflict at work, Margot doesn't jump in with solutions. She listens. "Do you want ideas," she asks, "or just someone to hear you out?"

Margot hasn't just become a better manager; she's become a more intentional person. She knows when to step in, when to coach, when to support, and when to let go. She thinks before she acts. She listens before she leads. She meets people where they are—at work, at home, and everywhere in between.

And as Chris McLean wrote so eloquently in his heartfelt foreword, that's what happens when Situational Leadership® becomes more than a model. It becomes a mindset, a way of moving through the world that's grounded in awareness, empathy, and choice.

Living the Model

Leadership isn't limited to the workplace; it's all around us. It happens in every sphere of life, from the personal to the professional. It shows up in classrooms and communities, in families and friendships, in boardrooms and break rooms. The same principles that helped Margot transform her team can reshape how any of us approach influence, in any arena.

A parent who pauses to diagnose before correcting discovers that defiance might actually be uncertainty. A teacher who adapts for a struggling student rebuilds confidence. A coach who communicates with empathy finds that feedback lands with empowerment instead of resistance. A project manager who adjusts structure as readiness grows creates autonomy. A mentor who asks rather than tells helps someone uncover their own wisdom.

Wherever it's applied, the truths remain the same: People are people, situations shift, and the ability to pause, diagnose, and respond intentionally determines whether others succeed or struggle.

When people are given what they need to succeed, performance improves. But something deeper happens too. Individuals thrive. Teams strengthen. Organizations grow. And along the way, we experience more joy, purpose, and meaning in our work. Because when people succeed, *everyone* wins.

Situational Leaders are others-focused. They think before they act. They don't lead by habit; they lead with awareness. Imagine a world—of workplaces, classrooms, families, even governments—where people paused long enough to consider what others truly need before responding. That's the power of this mindset. That's what it means to live the model.

Situational Leadership® works because it reflects what's true about people: We all grow, change, and respond differently depending on the situation. When we understand that, we stop managing from assumption and start leading with awareness. And when that awareness becomes habit, we don't just lead better; we *live* better. We become more present, more curious, more attuned to others, and more capable of responding in ways that build genuine connection and help people become better versions of themselves.

That's the power of the Situational Leadership® framework when it's lived, not just learned. It reminds us that leadership is all about connection. It's about awareness and action, working together in real time. And when we lead this way, when we meet people where they are and help them take the next step, we create an impact that lasts.

A Call to Practice

In the words of Hersey, "Theory and insight can give you great things to think about. The Situational Leadership® Model gives you practical things to do." So we end where we began: with a call to practice.

Leadership, like sport or art, can't be learned from pages alone. Principles become power only when you put them to work. So lead. Try the model the next time you need to influence. Walk the steps: Pause to diagnose, adapt your approach, communicate with intention, and help the work move forward. Notice what changes. Learn. Adjust. Begin again.

Some days you'll get it right; some days you won't. When you miss, repair. If trust is broken, rebuild it. If you chose the wrong style, own it and try again. Keep showing up. Keep choosing the response the moment requires. Over time your influence will shape results, strengthen engagement, and lift the people around you.

So in honor of our team at The Center for Leadership Studies, go lead.

Acknowledgments

As we mentioned in the dedication, and reiterated throughout, this book would not have been possible without the combined efforts of a dedicated CLS collective over time. In full view of that undeniable reality, we would like to thank our board, every member of our CLS team, our customers, our master trainers, and our global partners for their ongoing support and contributions.

Appendix

This appendix contains additional tools and resources for you to achieve more depth in the Situational Leadership® mindset and apply it in your real life. You can use these tools to start conversations about leadership with your team, your next-level leaders, or peers.

Situational Leadership®

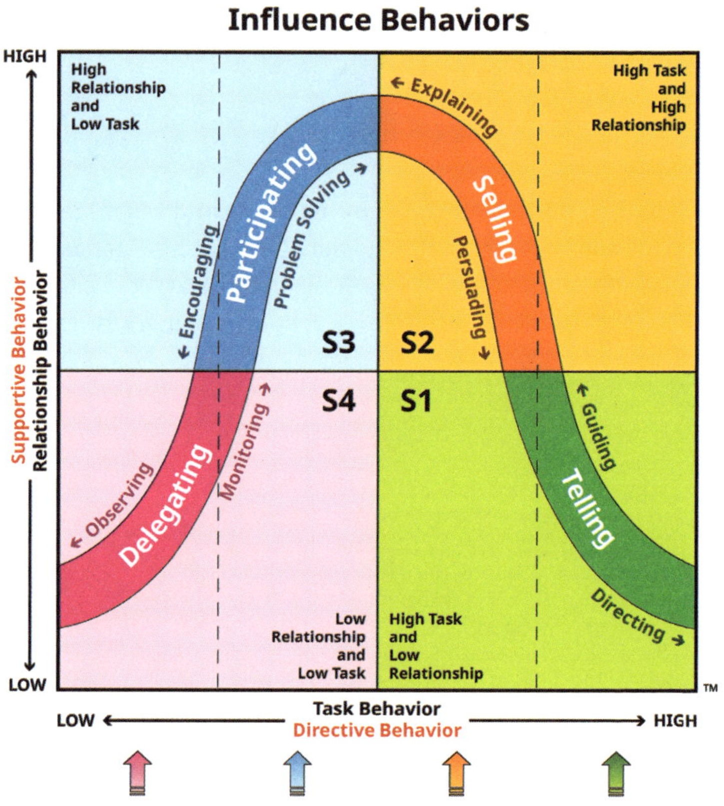

Performance Readiness®

HIGH	MODERATE		LOW
R4	**R3**	**R2**	**R1**
Able and Confident and Willing ←	Able but Insecure → or Unwilling	Unable but Confident ← or Willing	Unable and Insecure → or Unwilling

Self Directed   Leader Directed

Using Situational Leadership®

Step 1 | *Identify the specific task.*

Step 2 | *Assess current Performance Readiness®.*

Is the person currently performing at a sustained, acceptable level?
(Complex or not sure? Break task into smaller activities.)

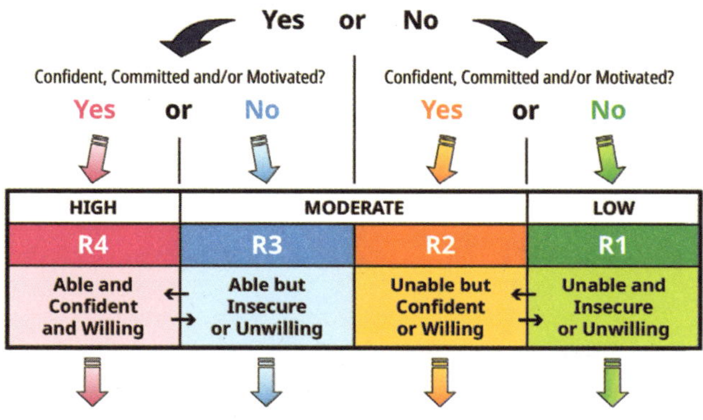

Step 3 | *Match and communicate leader response.*

What leadership response best meets the needs of the person?

Step 4 | *Manage the movement.*

What do I need to do to develop the individual's task performance or to prevent task performance from regressing?

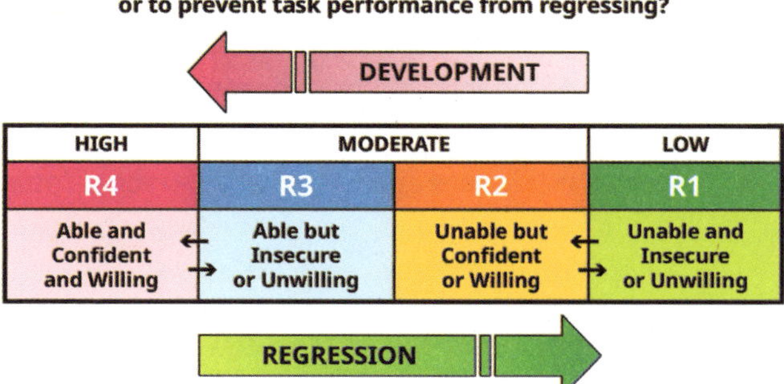

Characteristics of a Leader

Effective leadership is personal and purposeful—applicable to any situation. As practitioners, Situational Leaders reliably exhibit and fine-tune certain characteristics as identified from decades of working with some of the most effective leaders around the world. Examine the traits below that you currently embody for optimal execution and commit to grow those that are new or still developing.

Purpose-Driven

- Achieves alignment on vision, strategy, and execution
- Sets clear goals and holds people accountable for results
- Instills a sense of ownership that inspires commitment

Self-Aware

- Understands and manages how their emotions influence their behavior
- Recognizes how their behavior affects others' feelings and actions
- Practices empathy to appreciate and acknowledge others' experiences and feelings

Trustworthy

- Engages in honest and transparent communication
- Follows through on decisions and commitments
- Keeps confidences and maintains personal integrity

People-Centric

- Focuses on developing and supporting others' success and engagement
- Flexes and adapts to give others what they need when they need it
- Supports team members' health, well-being, and work-life balance

Humble

- Seeks feedback for self-improvement
- Admits mistakes or shortcomings
- Recognizes their strengths and weaknesses

Effective Communicator

- Cultivates personal connections and genuine relationships
- Engages in clear, open communication that facilitates collaboration
- Actively listens so others feel heard and valued

Learning Agility

- Embraces opportunities to stretch out of their comfort zone
- Leverages lessons learned and past experiences to navigate uncertainty
- Fosters a learning mindset to promote creativity and innovation

Respectful and Inclusive

- Creates a safe environment to share opinions or concerns without judgment or criticism
- Distributes fair and consistent recognition, rewards, and consequences
- Models and sets expectations for acceptance, unity, and mutual respect

Application Plan

Team member to influence:

STEP 1: IDENTIFY THE SPECIFIC TASK

Identify one task on which to focus.
Consider using a task where there is room for continuing performance improvement or where you have identified signs of performance regression.

STEP 2: ASSESS CURRENT PERFORMANCE READINESS®

Ability: Is the individual currently performing at a sustained, acceptable level?
Remember, for ability, the question is, "Are they?" and not, "Can they?"   ☐ **Yes**   ☐ **No**

What behaviors have you observed that support your assessment of ability?

Willingness: Is the individual confident, committed, and motivated for the task?
To determine an overall assessment for willingness, consider each element individually. Even if only one question is answered by indicating "no," that area may be the individual's strongest-felt need and may be enough for you to assess the individual as insecure or unwilling.

Confident: ☐ **Yes**   ☐ **No**   Committed: ☐ **Yes**   ☐ **No**   Motivated: ☐ **Yes**   ☐ **No**

Overall assessment: ☐ **Insecure or Unwilling**   ☐ **Confident or Willing**

What behaviors have you observed that support your assessment of willingness?

Make an initial assessment of their current Performance Readiness® for the task.

☐ R4	☐ R3	☐ R2	☐ R1

Select the leadership style that is a match for the individual's Performance Readiness®.

☐ S4	☐ S3	☐ S2	☐ S1

STEP 3: MATCH AND COMMUNICATE LEADER RESPONSE

How will you open the discussion to set the tone?

How will you describe current performance for the task?

Describe the task or directive leadership style behaviors you will demonstrate to meet the individual's needs.

Describe the relationship or supportive leadership style behaviors you will demonstrate to meet the individual's needs.

STEP 4: MANAGE THE MOVEMENT

Determine your next steps for this individual to advance development or reverse regression.

Describe how you will monitor and reinforce progress.

Conversation Starters to Advance Your Leadership Skills

Perhaps you have an upcoming discussion with a direct report and would like to gain insight into their leadership strengths, tendencies, or developmental areas. Or maybe you'd like to host a group discussion or simply self-reflect on your own effectiveness as a leader. Whatever the scenario, the questions in this guide can be used to stimulate meaningful discussion and insight into the behaviors used to influence others.

As a leader, it's important to recognize that effective leadership is an iterative, lifelong practice. Although some people may naturally have some of the instincts of a leader, no great leader is successful without making thoughtful, purposeful attempts to hone the necessary skills and characteristics required to lead situationally, with intention.

Leadership Characteristics

- As a leader, what leadership characteristics are most important to you?
- As a follower, what are the characteristics you look for in your leaders?
- What are the common themes or distinctions between what you expect from your leaders and the characteristics that are important to you as a leader?
- Do you have peers that you consider to be effective leaders? If yes, what characteristics or behaviors do they exhibit that make them so effective?
- When you consider your direct reports that stand out as leaders, what leadership characteristics do you think are their greatest strengths?

Leadership Self-Reflection

- How would you want people to describe you as a leader?
- Have you completed a formal assessment of your leadership behaviors (e.g., LEAD Self/LEAD Other)? If yes, how were others' perceptions of your leadership style the same as yours? How were they different? Were you surprised by any of the results?
- What are your greatest strengths as a leader?
- What do you think are your greatest challenges when leading others?
- What skills do you feel you could improve to be a more effective leader? What steps are you taking to develop in that area?
- How do you personally measure your success or effectiveness as a leader?

Achieving Same-Page Status

- Would your team members say that you are consistently aware of their priorities and tasks? Why or why not?
- What is your personal level of familiarity or experience with your team members' tasks? How does that influence your ability to achieve alignment on task expectations?
- Describe any successes or challenges you've experienced with gaining task-specific alignment and clarity.

Evaluating a Follower's Performance

- How effectively do you distinguish between ability and capability (or potential)?
- Have you ever misdiagnosed enthusiasm or confidence for ability? If yes, what was the situation, and what did you learn from the experience?

- When assessing an individual's Performance Readiness® for a task, how do you determine their confidence, commitment, and motivation? What indicators do you look for?
- Describe any successes or challenges you've experienced when attempting to diagnose an individual's strongest-felt need.

Adapting Your Leadership Style

- When making the conscious and intentional decision about how to respond to a situation, what adjustments do you consider based on your preferred leadership style?
- What questions could you ask to gain alignment with the performer on their ability for a task?
- What questions could you ask to gain alignment with the performer on their willingness for a task?
- Reflect on your personal preferences and tendencies as a leader. What adjustments might you make to increase your flexibility and adaptability across the four styles?
- Can you think of a situation in which you underled, giving the follower support but not enough direction for a task? If yes, describe the situation and what you learned from the experience.
- Can you think of a situation in which you overled, giving a performer too much direction or structure and not enough support for a task? If yes, describe the situation and what you learned from the experience.
- When you want to communicate a leader-directed style, how do you set the tone for the conversation in the first thirty seconds?
- When you want to communicate a performer-driven style, how do you set the tone for the conversation in the first thirty seconds?
- Have you ever recognized in the moment that your leadership style was not a match? If yes, what did you do? What did you learn from the experience?

- How do you prepare to communicate a leadership style that is less comfortable or intuitive to you? What do you do to stretch out of your comfort zone?

Managing the Movement

- Situational Leaders recognize that shifts in ability and willingness are inevitable. How do you stay in tune with team members' changing circumstances and performance needs? Are there any opportunities to improve communication frequency or effectiveness with your team members?
- If your team is hybrid or remote, do you see potential barriers to communication and connection that should be addressed?
- Describe any successes or challenges you've experienced when implementing practices to foster development among your team.
- Can you think of a situation where a team member's performance for a task was regressing? If yes, what did you do, and how did you know when to step in?
- Are you currently seeing any signs of regression among your team members? If yes, what do they look like?
- Describe any successes or challenges you've experienced when attempting to reverse regression.

Diagnostic Questions

Use the diagnostic questions below based on the level of familiarity and trust you have built with the follower. As you continue to build a relationship around the work with this individual, you will be able to ask more in-depth questions, but it's important to respect the performer's boundaries. These questions are written to help you weave in external considerations that may be affecting the performer.

Low Trust

- How are you handling [specific organizational change]? Do you have any concerns?
- How are you settling into your new role? Do you have any concerns?
- What do you need to perform at your best?
- Do you have conflicting priorities that are making it difficult for you to perform?
- Do you feel we have same-page status on the task?
- What do you foresee being the most challenging aspect of this task?
- How have the changes in the team or organization affected you and your tasks?

Moderate Trust

- Is there anything on your mind that's making it difficult for you to fully engage at work?
- How do you feel about working with [team member] on this?
- What don't I know about your day-to-day that would help me lead you better?
- What do you think might be impeding your development on this task?
- If I could remove one stressor from your workday to enable you to be more successful, what would it be?

High Trust

- How are things going outside work?
- I've noticed that you seem disengaged at work lately. Is there any context you want to share with me?

- I understand if [specific personal change] is making it difficult for you to concentrate on work. How can I support you so that we can still hit our goals?
- I've noticed some tension between you and [team member]. Would you be willing to share what might be causing that so we can get to the root of the issue and all work together better?

Questions to Ask Your Leader During Change

- When are we kicking off this change?
- When can I start sharing information with my team?
- Why are we doing this change?
- What made you decide on this approach?
- Do you know of any examples of organizations that have gone through similar changes that I can look into?
- What are the goals of the change?
- How does this change tie into our organizational goals?
- What do you see as my team's role in this change?
- Should I expect any personnel changes on my team as a result of this change?
- How will you measure the success of my team in this change?
- What can I do in advance to prepare my team for this change?
- What cross-functional collaboration do you think will be a part of this change?
- Who is going to be most affected by this change?
- What skills do you think will be most valuable in making this change a success?
- How do you think my team's day-to-day tasks will change because of this?
- Will these change-related tasks be a higher priority than our existing tasks?
- How should I share my teams concerns with you?

- What are your concerns in implementing this change?
- Is there anything you've shared with me that I should not share with my team?

Authors' Note and Related References

When we committed to writing this book, we agreed to present the *Situational Leadership*® Model using a hybrid approach. We intended the book to fall between two previous publications written by Dr. Hersey:

- *The Situational Leader* (Hersey, Paul. *The Situational Leader.* The Center for Leadership Studies, 1984.)
- *Management of Organizational Behavior* (Hersey, Paul H., Kenneth H. Blanchard, and Dewey E. Johnson. Pearson, 2012.)

The Situational Leader was a fable published in the mid-1980s that chronicled a first-time leader learning how to become more effective. The experiences of Margot, Joshua, Hana, and Priya in this book recount similar journeys.

Management of Organizational Behavior was first published as *The Life Cycle Theory of Leadership* in 1969. It became the best-selling organizational behavior text of its time and was updated through each of its ten editions. Our discussion of power, the model, leadership competencies, the four steps, performance management, and change is grounded in the depth of the book's eighth edition.

We are frequently asked this question:

- Why has Situational Leadership® withstood the test of time?

From our perspective it is akin to asking how the pyramids in Egypt could possibly still be upright and vibrant centuries after their creation—it has everything to do with the strength of their foundation.

Over twenty pioneering research studies formed the foundation for Situational Leadership®. Chapters 3 and 4 ("The Origins of Leadership Styles" and "The Roots of Readiness") highlight the studies we believe are most critical. And not surprisingly, much of this research has been pulled through in various ways to the present. Here is a representative sample of that work.

Taylor, Frederick W. *The Principles of Scientific Management.* Harper & Brothers, 1911.

Bell, Reginald L., and Jeanette S. Martin. "The Relevance of Scientific Management and Equity Theory in Everyday Managerial Communication Situations." *Journal of Management Policy and Practice* 13, no. 3 (2012): 106–15.

Turan, Hakan. "Taylor's Scientific Management Principles: Contemporary Issues in Personnel Selection Period." *Journal of Economics, Business and Management* 3, no. 11 (2015): 1102–05.

Uddin, Nasir, and Fariha Hossain. "Evolution of Modern Management Through Taylorism: An Adjustment of Scientific Management Comprising Behavioral Science." *Procedia Computer Science* 62 (2015): 578–84.

Savino, David. "Frederick Winslow Taylor and His Lasting Legacy of Functional Leadership Competence." *Journal of Leadership, Accountability and Ethics* 13, no. 1 (2016): 70–76.

O'Neill, Christopher. "Taylorism, the European Science of Work, and the Quantified Self at Work." *Science, Technology, & Human Values* 42, no. 4 (2017): 600–21.

Mayo, Elton. *The Social Problems of an Industrial Civilization.* Harvard Business School, 1945.

Rotich, Jacob Kipkemboi. "History, Evolution and Development of Human Resource Management: A Contemporary Perspective." *Global Journal of Human Resource Management* 3, no. 3 (2015): 58–73.

Williams, Joan C., and Sky Mihaylo. "How the Best Bosses Interrupt Bias on Their Teams." *Harvard Business Review* 97, no. 6 (2019): 151–55.

Akintokunbo, Oluwarotimi Odunayo, and Ebere Chika John-Eke. "The Alignment of Employee Engagement with Human Relations School of Thought." *American Journal of Humanities and Social Sciences Research* 5, no. 9 (2021): 99–106.

Tulshyan, Ruchika, and Jodi-Ann Burey. "Stop Telling Women They Have Imposter Syndrome." *Harvard Business Review* (2021).

Brown, Brené. Interview with Ruchika Tulshyan. "Inclusion on Purpose." *Dare to Lead*, April 25, 2022. Podcast, Spotify, 1:12:00.

Brown, Brené. "The Heart of Daring Leadership." *Dare to Lead*, October 2020. Podcast, Spotify, 41:16.

Stogdill, Ralph M., and Alvin Coons, eds. *Leader Behavior: Its Description and Measurement, Research Monograph No. 88*. Bureau of Business Research, Ohio State University, 1957.

McClesky, Jim Allen. "Situational, Transformational, and Transactional Leadership and Leadership Development." *Journal of Business Studies Quarterly* 5, no. 4 (2014): 117–30.

James, Erika H., and Lynn Perry Wooten. *The Prepared Leader: Emerge from Any Crisis More Resilient than Before*. Wharton School Press, 2022.

Brown, Brené. Interview with Erika James and Lynn Perry Wooten. "The Prepared Leader, 1 of 2." *Dare to Lead*, September 2022. Podcast, Spotify, 45:27.

Brown, Brené. Interview with Erika James and Lynn Perry Wooten. "The Prepared Leader, 2 of 2." *Dare to Lead*, September 2022. Podcast, Spotify, 35:59.

McGregor, Douglas. *The Human Side of Enterprise.* McGraw-Hill, 1960.

Sinek, Simon. *Start with Why: How Great Leaders Inspire Everyone to Take Action.* Penguin Group, Inc., 2009.

Elliot, Andrew J., and Carol S. Dweck. *Handbook of Competence and Motivation.* Guilford, 2013.

Sinek, Simon. *Leaders Eat Last: Why Some Teams Pull Together and Others Don't.* Penguin Group, LLC, 2014.

Dweck, Carol S., and David S. Yeager. "Mindsets: A View from Two Eras." *Perspectives on Psychological Science* 14, no. 3 (2019): 481–96.

Fancher, Sarah E. "Radical Empathy and the Managerial Ethic of Care." *Academic Librarian Burnout: Causes and Response* (2023): 233–42.

Argyris, Chris. *Interpersonal Competence and Organizational Effectiveness.* Irwin-Dorsey Press, 1962.

Buckingham, Marcus, and Ashley Goodall. "The Feedback Fallacy." *Harvard Business Review* 97, no. 2 (2019): 92–101.

Buckingham, Marcus, and Ashley Goodall. "Reinventing Performance Management." *Harvard Business Review* 93, no. 4 (2015): 40–50.

Ingram, Paul, and Yoonjin Choi. "What Does Your

Company Really Stand For?" *Harvard Business Review* 100, no. 6 (2022): 40–47.

Quinn, Robert E., and Anjan V. Thakor. "Creating a Purpose-Driven Organization." *Harvard Business Review* 96, no. 4 (2018): 78–85.

Maslow, Abraham H. *Motivation and Personality.* Harper & Row, 1954.

Harvard, Phillip S. "Maslow, Mazes, Minotaurs: Updating Employee Needs and Behavior Patterns in a Knowledge-Based Global Economy." *Journal of the Knowledge Economy* 1 (2010): 117–27.

Pink, Daniel H. *Drive: The Surprising Truth About What Motivates Us.* Canongate Books, 2011.

Morgan, John H. "The Personal Meaning of Social Values in the Work of Abraham Maslow." *Interpersona: An International Journal on Personal Relationships* 6, no. 1 (2012): 75–93.

Zomorodi, Manoush. "Maslow's Human Needs." *TED Radio Hour*, April 2015. Podcast, National Public Radio.

Dar, Showkat Ahmad, and P. Sakthivel. "Maslow's Hierarchy of Needs Is Still Relevant in the 21st Century." *Journal of Learning and Educational Policy* 2, no. 5 (2022).

Kaufman, Scott Barry. "Abraham Maslow and the Science of Self-Actualization." *New Thinking Allowed Podcast*, August 2025. Podcast, Apple Podcasts.

Herzberg, Frederick, Bernard Mausner, and Barbara Snyderman. *The Motivation to Work.* John Wiley & Sons, 1959.

Buckingham, Marcus, and Curt Coffman. *First, Break All the Rules.* Gallup Press, 1999.

O'Boyle, Ed. *4 Things Gen Z and Millennials Expect from Their Workplace.* Gallup, 2021.

Buckingham, Marcus. "Designing Work That People Love." *Harvard Business Review,* 100, no. 3 (2022): 66–75.

Berger, Laura. *Managing Millennials in the Workplace.* Forbes, 2020.

Bhatt, Nishant, Jaya Chitranshi, and Mita Mehta. "Testing Herzberg's Two Factor Theory on Millennials." *Cardiometry* 22 (2022): 231–36.

Kulkarni, Abha, Susan K. Hogan, Steve Hatfield, and Roxana Corduneanu. "Millennials and the 'Staying Power' of Pay." Deloitte Insights, 2022.

About The Center for Leadership Studies

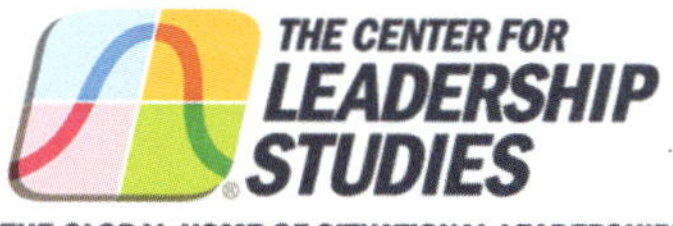

The Center for Leadership Studies (CLS) is committed to enabling leaders at all levels to achieve their highest potential through innovative, impactful leadership training that is grounded in research and application. As the global home of the Situational Leadership® Model, the most successful and widely adopted leadership model available, CLS's award-winning solutions enable leaders to engage in effective performance conversations that build trust, increase productivity, and drive behavior change.

The organization's foundation was built on a comprehensive analysis of the pioneering contributions that shaped the field leadership. This research informed the creation of the Situational Leadership® Model, and decades of application have continued to validate its strength.

Connect with The Center for Leadership Studies

Endnotes

1   *State of the Global Workplace Report*. Gallup, 15 June 2021, www.gallup.
     com/workplace/349484/state-of-the-global-workplace.aspx.

2   https://www.linkedin.com/in/marshallgoldsmith/.

3   Harari, Oren. *Quotations from Chairman Powell: A Leadership Primer*.
     GovLeaders.org, 1996, govleaders.org/powell.php.

4   Solomon, Lou. *Two-Thirds of Managers Are Uncomfortable Communicating
     with Employees*. Harvard Business Review, 16 Mar. 2016, https://hbr.
     org/2016/03/two-thirds-of-managers-are-uncomfortable-communicating-
     with-employees.

5   *State of the American Manager Report*. Gallup, 2015, https://www.gallup.
     com/services/182138/state-american-manager.aspx.

6   *2024 Pulse of Change Index*. Accenture, 2024, https://www.accenture.
     com/content/dam/accenture/final/accenture-com/document-2/Accenture-
     Pulse-of-Change-2024-Index-Executive-Summary.pdf.

7   Turner, J. *This New Strategy Could Be Your Ticket to Change Management
     Success*. Gartner, 28 Nov. 2022, https://www.gartner.com/en/articles/
     this-new-strategy-could-be-your-ticket-to-change-management-success.

8   Bucy, Michael, et al. *Losing from Day One: Why Even Successful
     Transformations Fall Short*. McKinsey & Company, 7 Dec. 2021, www.
     mckinsey.com/capabilities/people-and-organizational-performance/
     our-insights/successful-transformations.

About the Authors

Sam Shriver is the executive vice president at The Center for Leadership Studies and a proud graduate of the United States Coast Guard Academy. He received his MBA from Pepperdine University and his PhD from North Carolina State University. He has been a contributor to the training industry for more than forty-five years. *Situational Leadership®* is his fifth book. He currently lives in Raleigh, North Carolina, is an active member of the Legatus organization, and reports to six grandchildren.

Suzie Bishop is the vice president of product development at The Center for Leadership Studies, where she drives innovative and experiential learning solutions to better equip leaders for the modern workplace. She is an expert in the Situational Leadership® framework, a member of Marshall Goldsmith's 100 Coaches community, and a columnist for *Training Industry Magazine.* She was recognized as an Elliott Masie 30 Under 30 leader.